Inventing the Truth

JimNECHAS

Inventing the Truth

THE ART AND CRAFT
OF MEMOIR

REVISED AND EXPANDED SECOND EDITION

RUSSELL BAKER / JILL KER CONWAY

ANNIE DILLARD / IAN FRAZIER

HENRY LOUIS GATES, JR. / ALFRED KAZIN

TONI MORRISON / EILEEN SIMPSON

Edited with an Introduction by
WILLIAM ZINSSER

HOUGHTON MIFFLIN COMPANY
BOSTON   NEW YORK

Introduction, copyright © 1987 and 1995 by William K. Zinsser.
Life With Mother, copyright © 1987 by Russell Baker. *To Fashion a
Text,* copyright © 1987 by Annie Dillard. *The Past Breaks Out,*
copyright © 1987 by Alfred Kazin. *The Site of Memory,* copyright
© 1987 by Toni Morrison. *Poets in My Youth,* copyright © 1995
by Eileen Simpson. *Looking for My Family,* copyright © 1995 by
Ian Frazier. *Lifting the Veil,* copyright © 1995 by Henry Louis
Gates, Jr. *Points of Departure,* copyright © 1995 by Jill Ker Conway.

For information about permission to reproduce selections from
this book, write to Permissions, Houghton Mifflin Company,
215 Park Avenue South, New York, New York 10003.

For information about this and other Houghton Mifflin
trade and reference books and multimedia products, visit
The Bookstore at Houghton Mifflin on the World Wide Web
at http://www.hmco.com.trade/.

Library of Congress Cataloguing-in-Publication Data
Inventing the truth : the art and craft of memoir / Russell Baker
... [et al.] ; edited by William Zinsser. — Rev. and expanded.
      p.   cm.
   Includes bibliographical references (p.   ).
   ISBN 0-395-73101-1
      1. Autobiography.   2. United States — Biography —
History and criticism.   3. Authors, American — 20th century
— Biography — History and criticism.   I. Baker, Russell,
1925–   . II. Zinsser, William Knowlton.
CT25.158   1995   95-17169
920.073 — dc20   CIP

Contents

WILLIAM ZINSSER

Introduction

In the early 1960s I was invited to write one-fifth of a book. It was called *Five Boyhoods*, and it consisted of memoirs written by five men who grew up in successive decades of the twentieth century. The first chapter, by Howard Lindsay, described his turn-of-the-century boyhood in Atlantic City, a sunny Victorian world not much different from the one he would inhabit many years later as coauthor and star of one of Broadway's longest-running plays, *Life with Father*. The second chapter ("1910s"), by Harry Golden, evoked a world as cramped as Lindsay's was spacious: the dark ghetto of immigrant Jews on New York's Lower East Side. Chapter 3, on the 1920s, was by Walt Kelly, who belonged to an Irish clan that seemed to be in perpetual migration between Bridgeport and Philadelphia — hardly the twenties of F. Scott Fitzgerald's "Jazz Age," but could Fitzgerald have created Pogo? My chapter ("1930s") was about a boyhood spent in a vale of prosperous WASPs on the north shore of Long Island, and the fifth chapter, by John Updike, recalled what it was like to grow up in the 1940s as the only child of schoolteachers in a small town in Pennsylvania. Updike's father, haunted by the fear of poverty, was glad the family lived next to a poorhouse; if necessary he could walk there.

Five boyhoods, as unalike as American boyhoods could be. Yet what struck me about the five accounts was how many themes they had in common. One was loneliness, the universal plight. Another was humor, the universal solvent. I also saw that memory, that powerful writer's tool, can be highly unreliable: The boy's remembered truth was often different from his parents' remembered truth. My mother, after reading my chapter, cried because my memory of my boyhood was less golden than *her* memory of my boyhood. Had I subconsciously reinvented it to make it more lonely than it really was? Had she subconsciously never noticed?

Mine was the most privileged of the five boyhoods. In 1920 my parents had built a large and agreeable house — one of those summery, white-shingled houses with many screened porches — on four acres of hilly land near the end of King's Point, overlooking Manhasset Bay and Long Island Sound. Boats and water were my view; I thought it was as beautiful a location for a home as any boy could ask for. My father's business in New York withstood the Depression, so my three sisters and I were sheltered from its cold winds, and we grew up in a happy family, well loved and well provided for.

But the beautiful house was two miles from the nearest

town and not near any other house. I wanted to live on a block, like everybody else, doing block things. I was also the only boy for miles around. By some Mendelian fluke, no boys had been born to any of the nearby families. It was a neighborhood of girls, and that's what our house was full of: my sisters and their friends, giggling over girlish secrets, talking a language laden with mysteries. One of the first words I can remember hearing was "organdy." What did it mean? I never knew and never dared to ask.

Outflanked, I escaped into baseball. Once I entered that world of flanneled heroes I thought about little else. Sometimes during the long summers I tried to dragoon the girls into playing ball. I was a proto–Charlie Brown, ever optimistic that they would catch a fly hit in their direction or throw a runner out. But no runner got thrown out. I learned very early the fact that girls "throw funny." They explained that it was because their arms are "set different." Was that an anatomical fact, or just another strand in the folklore of growing up, like saltpeter in the school food and poison at the center of the golf ball? Whatever the truth, I was stuck with the result.

So began the solitary ballgames that were to occupy much of my youth. Every day I threw a tennis ball for hours against the side of our house, adroitly fielding with a glove the line drives and grounders that sprang out of the quivering shingles, impersonating whole major league teams and keeping elaborate box scores. Little did my parents, trapped inside their booming home, realize that the person out there on the grass wasn't me. That impeccable stylist at second base was Charlie Gehringer of the

Detroit Tigers; that gazelle in the outfield was Joe Di-Maggio. If my family had only looked out the window they could have seen greatness.

Being a baseball addict in those days was harder work than it is today. Television hadn't been born, and games weren't even broadcast on the radio. When I was nine my parents sent me to a summer camp on Cape Cod, hoping I might develop a fondness for canoeing or some other, less tyrannical sport. But one day at camp I made a great discovery: An announcer named Fred Hoey on a Boston radio station did play-by-play accounts of all the home games of the Red Sox and the Braves. How idyllic, I thought, to live near Boston; no wonder it was called the Athens of America. For years afterward I fiddled with my radio dial, trying to bring Hoey's voice through the atmosphere to my bedside Philco. Once I thought I heard him, very faintly.

In such a deprived climate I subsisted on the printed word. At breakfast I gorged myself on the baseball articles and box scores in the *New York Herald Tribune* and the *New York Times*. In the evening I waited for my father to come home so that I could grab his *New York Sun*, a paper as baseball-crazed as I was, and in between I would reread copies of *Baseball* magazine, to which I subscribed, or study with monkish dedication what was fast becoming the biggest Big League Gum collection in the East. It was from those wonderful baseball writers that I first glimpsed what it might mean to be a newspaperman; they were my first "influence," the mentors who nudged me down the path to my life's work.

But the memoir I wrote for *Five Boyhoods* was only indirectly about my obsession with baseball. It was really the story of a boy contending with certain kinds of isolation. Size was another isolating factor. I was the smallest of boys, late to grow, living in a society of girls who shot up like mutants and were five-foot-nine by the age of twelve. Nowhere was the disparity sharper than at the dances I was made to attend throughout my youth. The tribal rules required every boy to bring a gardenia to the girl who had invited him, which she would pin to the bosom of her gown. Too young to appreciate the bosom, I was just tall enough for my nose to be pressed into the gardenia I had brought to adorn it. The sickly smell of that flower was like chloroform as I lurched round and round the dance floor. Talk was almost out of the question; my lofty partner was just as isolated and resentful. What I remember about those nights is the quality of time standing still. I thought they would never end.

In *Five Boyhoods* I cloaked these unhappy memories in humor — an old habit. Humor is the writer's armor against hard emotions — and therefore, in the case of memoir, one more distortion of the truth. Probably I also used humor as a kindness to my family. When I started writing that memoir I was half paralyzed by the awareness that my parents and my sisters were looking over my shoulder, if not actually perched there, and would read whatever version of their life came out of my typewriter. My first drafts were stiff, and though the style became warmer with each rewrite, I never really relaxed and enjoyed it. Since then, reading other memoirs, I've wondered how many passengers were along on the ride, subtly altering the past.

My grandmother, my father's mother, was a stern presence in our lives. A second-generation American, she hadn't lost the Germanic relish for telling people off, and she had many didactic maxims to reinforce her point. "Kalt Kaffee macht schön," she would declare, wagging her forefinger, leaving us to deconstruct the dreadful message. "Cold coffee makes beautiful," it said, as if hot coffee were some kind of self-indulgence, or perhaps a known cause of ugliness. "Morgen Stund hat Gold im Mund" ("The morning hour has gold in its mouth") she would say to grandchildren who slept late. Frida Zinsser was a woman of fierce pride, bent on cultural improvement for herself and her family — she hectored my father and his brother Rudolph to play the piano and the violin with her long after they had lost interest in those instruments — and in my memoir I duly noted her strength. But I also made it clear that she was no fun.

After *Five Boyhoods* came out my mother tried to set me straight. "Grandma really wasn't like that," she said, defending the mother-in-law who had made her own life far from easy. "She was unhappy and really quite shy, and she very much wanted to be liked." Maybe so; the truth is somewhere between my mother's version and mine. But she was like that to *me* — and that's the only truth that a memoir writer can work with.

All else being subjective, I probably got only one part of my memoir "right" — objectively accurate to all the principal players — and that was the part about the much-loved house and the site it occupied. I described the house, with its sunlit rooms and its pleasant porches that enabled us to watch an endless armada of boats: sailboats, motorboats, excursion boats, launches, freighters, tankers, trawlers, tugs, barges, Navy destroyers, and, every night at six, one of the two night steamers of the Fall River Line — aging belles named the *Priscilla* and the *Commonwealth*. I described the sounds of the water that were threaded through our lives: the chime of a bell buoy, the mournful foghorn of Execution Light, the nighttime conversation of eelers fishing near the shore, the unsteady drone of an outboard motor, which, even more than the banging of a screen door, still means summer to me. I described the hill in front of our house that we sledded down on our Flexible Flyers. One winter Long Island Sound froze over and cars drove around on the ice.

A decade after World War II my parents began to find the house hard to manage, and they sold it and moved to Manhattan. By then quite a few of their grandchildren — my sisters' children — had played on those porches and watched those boats and listened to the foghorn at night. The house had become a homestead; another generation would remember it. I only went back to see it once, after my mother's funeral at the old family church. My own children were with me, and as I drove down the once-rural King's Point Road I could have been in any affluent suburb anywhere. The sloping fields that I remembered on both sides of the road were so dense with ranch houses and three-car garages and swimming pools that I had no sense of their topography. I only knew it in my bones.

At the end of the road, however, our house was still king of the hill. Someone had told me that it had changed hands over the years, and on this day it happened to be between occupants again. Only a contractor was there. She invited us in and showed us how the new owner had torn out much of the interior and was preparing to reincarnate it in Beverly Hills modern. Terrazzo squares were piled on the old wooden floors that they would soon cover; unassembled parts for several Jacuzzis awaited the plumber. Fair enough — I had no claim on the house. Its integrity was gone, but at least it was still there. I could tell my children, "This is the house I grew up in."

But the Jacuzzi man must have tired of his new palace. A few years later the house was up for sale again; my sister Nancy saw it advertised in the section of the *New York Times Magazine* that features "luxury estates." Later I heard that it had been bought by an Iranian. I wondered how much more improving the old house could take. Then, one day, an unexpected errand took me out to the family church. My wife, Caroline, was with me. I had an uneasy feeling about the house and didn't want to face finding out what had happened to it. But Caroline urged me to put the past to rest, and once again I pointed the car down King's Point Road.

At the end of the road I saw the two familiar stone gateposts and turned into our driveway. Something was missing: It was the house. Without the crowning house, the hill hardly seemed to be a hill. Had our Flexible Flyers hurtled down that mere incline? We walked up the former hill and stared into an enormous hole where the house had been. The entire place was unkempt; it looked as if it had been abandoned for many months. I could only guess that some Iranian holding company, having cleared the land, was holding it for development.

We walked around the big hole and went and sat on the seawall. It was a perfect July day. The waters of Manhasset Bay and Long Island Sound glittered in the summer sun, and there were boats as far as I could see: power boats and fishing boats and excursion boats, freighters and tugs and barges, and hundreds of sailboats strung out in a yacht club regatta. I heard a bell buoy and an outboard motor. I was at ease and only slightly sad. The beautiful view was intact: the unique configuration of sea and land I remember so well that I still dream about it.

But the house survived only as an act of writing.

This is a book by eight writers who have gone looking for their past with acts of writing. It originated in 1986 as a series of talks on "The Art and Craft of Memoir," conceived and sponsored by the Book-of-the-Month Club, where I was then working, and held at the New York Public Library. Memoir was defined as some portion of a life. Unlike autobiography, which moves in a dutiful line from birth to fame, omitting nothing, memoir assumes the life and ignores most of it. A memoir writer takes us back to a moment in his or her life that was unusually vivid, such as childhood, or that was framed by war or travel or some other exceptional event. By narrowing the lens, the writer achieves a focus that's not possible in autobiography. Memoir is a window into a life.

The original speakers were told that our interest was in "process." We didn't want authors lecturing about a genre;

we wanted writers talking about how they do what they do. That's what we got.

Russell Baker, the Pulitzer Prize–winning columnist of the *New York Times*, had recently written *Growing Up*, which was not only a superb memoir of his boyhood; it was a classic book about the Depression, perfectly demonstrating that a good memoir is also a work of history, catching a distinctive moment in the life of both a person and a society. Baker's story took tremendous strength from its national context of poverty and struggle.

Annie Dillard, author of *Pilgrim at Tinker's Creek*, was then completing a memoir called *An American Childhood*, in which she situated her lively Pittsburgh childhood in the larger framework of the American landscape, "the vast setting of our common history." Her memoir, she said, was about what it feels like to wake up and "notice that you've been set down in a going world."

Alfred Kazin, dean of American literary critics, had then written three memoirs about successive phases of his life, the richest being *A Walker in the City*, which dealt with his childhood as the son of immigrant Jews in Brooklyn. I still remember how sensual that memoir was. Kazin wrote with his nose, making me smell what his mother was cooking for the Sabbath dinner and how his father's overalls smelled of turpentine when he came home from his job as a housepainter.

Toni Morrison, a Nobel Prize–winning novelist, isn't usually identified with nonfiction writing. Yet her African-American heritage is a powerful current in her work. In books like *Song of Solomon* we hear voices far older than her own: fragments of handed-down language and lore that constitute the black oral tradition. "When I think of things my mother and father and aunts used to say," she once remarked, "it seems the most absolutely striking thing in the world."

All the talks were tape-recorded, and I worked from the transcripts to shape them into a book. The title *Inventing the Truth* was suggested by an insistent theme that kept bobbing up: that the writer of a memoir must become the editor of his or her own life, imposing a narrative pattern and an organizing idea on an unwieldy mass of half-remembered events. "The autobiographer's problem," said Russell Baker, "is that he knows too much; he knows the whole iceberg, not just the tip." Refining the point, Annie Dillard said, "The writer of any first-person work must decide two obvious questions: what to put in and what to leave out."

Even, mere distillation is no free pass to the reader's interest, as Russell Baker discovered when he wrote the first draft of *Growing Up*, using the reflexes of a lifelong journalist. What he wrote was "a reporter's book," recreating the Depression after interviewing some of his older relatives who lived through it. What he left out, with a reporter's propriety, was his mother and himself — in short, the story. That disastrous first version, he saw, not only had to be rewritten; it had to be reinvented. The result was a book about "an extremely strong woman and a weak male." How much of it was artifice? I only know that it felt true.

Toni Morrison, groping for truth in the buried past,

also knows that it can only be quarried by an act of imagination. She takes as her literary inheritance the narratives written by slaves in the eighteenth and nineteenth centuries to persuade white Americans that blacks were "worthy of God's grace and the immediate abandonment of slavery." But because they wanted to elevate the argument and not anger their masters, they "dropped a veil" over the terrible details of their daily existence; no trace of their thoughts or emotions can be found. Toni Morrison wants access to that interior life; it contains the truth about her past that she needs for her work. She can only get it by imagining it. Unlike Russell Baker, heightening reality to give it the drama of fiction, Toni Morrison uses fiction to discover what was real. Both of them have skipped over research and landed on the truth.

Putting all this in formal terms, Annie Dillard says, "My advice to memoir writers is to fashion a text." The advice sounds too academic; we like to think that an interesting life will fashion itself into a text. It won't. We like to think that Thoreau went back to Concord and just wrote up his notes. He didn't; he wrote seven drafts of *Walden* in eight years, piecing together by what Margaret Fuller called the "mosaic" method a book that seems casual and even chatty. Thoreau wasn't a woodsman when he went to the woods; he was a writer, and he wrote one of our sacred texts. When he was finished he had probably forgotten most of what he did at Walden Pond. If you prize your memories, don't write a memoir, Annie Dillard warns. The act of writing about a long-gone event is so much more intense than the experience itself that what you write becomes your remembered truth, just as the snapshots of your vacation become more real than your vacation. You have cannibalized your past and reinvented it.

For Alfred Kazin, the son of Russian Jews, memoir was the door he walked through to claim his American birthright — books such as *The Education of Henry Adams*, Thoreau's *Walden* and especially his journals, Ralph Waldo Emerson's journals and essays, and Walt Whitman's *Leaves of Grass* and his Civil War diary *Specimen Days*. What struck Kazin was how personal those writers were; they used the most intimate literary forms to place themselves in the fabric of American history. Those works brought Kazin the news that was to shape his life: "One could be a writer without writing a novel. Every taxi driver and bartender who told you his story wanted to be a novelist; it was the big thing in America." But it wasn't the big thing to Kazin. He recalls that Leslie Fiedler, reviewing *A Walker in the City*, found it perverse that the book "obstinately refuses to be a novel."

Personal history — memoirs, journals, diaries, letters — became the one true form for Kazin. The daily journal that he began writing as a boy was "a cherished connection with something fundamental to American literature — the need to present to God, the Eternal Reader and Judge of of the soul's pilgrimage on earth, the veritable record of one's inner life." Kazin took this Puritan "habit of mind" with him when he wrote *A Walker in the City* and its sequels, *Starting Out in the Thirties* and *New York Jew*.

With those memoirs he planted his roots next to those of his literary idols in the memoir-rich American soil.

So *Inventing the Truth* was born, and it has found favor ever since with writers and students trying to figure out how to tell their story. The book has also been popular with the growing number of high school and college teachers who teach courses in memoir writing, journal writing, and other personal forms. Every year more and more of them tell me how helpful the book is to them and to their students. It's helpful because it's anecdotal. Few books exist in which memoir writers talk about their attitudes and their decisions.

Suddenly it occurred to me that if a book so haphazardly born was so helpful, it could be much more helpful, and I decided to expand it by adding new writers. To preserve its spoken integrity I would go to the new writers with my tape recorder and ask them to tell me how they wrote their memoirs. By my choice of writers and by the nature of my questions I would elicit certain points about memoir writing that I wanted to have in this edition and that weren't covered earlier. Later I would edit myself out of the conversation.

I began by making a list of writers and reducing it to five, the first of whom, Eudora Welty, author of *One Writer's Beginnings*, turned me down for reasons I couldn't argue with. "It's the doing of it that does it," she explained, placing herself, epigrammatically, in the sizable company of artists who prefer to let their work speak for itself.

Fortunately, the other four writers — Eileen Simpson, Ian Frazier, Henry Louis Gates, Jr., and Jill Ker Conway — agreed to go along on the ride. I also reluctantly dropped one of the original riders: Lewis Thomas, author of *Lives of a Cell*. In his talk Dr. Thomas took his listeners on a backward journey of unimaginable length, nothing less than a memoir of life on earth. It was an elegant high-wire act, but it wouldn't tell an individual member of that long line of cells how to write a memoir today.

The four new writers in this edition represent four powerful types of memoir, all new to *Inventing the Truth*.

Eileen Simpson represents all the memoir writers who incur what they know will be considerable pain to repossess their past. For *Poets in Their Youth*, a memoir of her life with her first husband, John Berryman, and his famously self-destructive fellow poets, Simpson had to revisit the collapse of that marriage and the dazzling world it was built on. To write *Orphans*, which recalls her upbringing without parents, she did historical research on orphanhood that became so traumatic that she abandoned the book several times. For *Reversals* she had to reveal the lifelong shame, carefully hidden as an adult, of having been a dyslexic child, the class dunce, unable to read, in the days before dyslexia was understood. What saved her in each case was the knowledge, learned in her separate career as a psychotherapist, that the past is best confronted — a good lesson for all memoir writers apprehensive about opening Pandora's box. Once she even used her analyst's technique on herself, lying on a couch to summon back a weekend spent thirty years earlier with Robert Lowell and Jean Stafford. "It was like waiting under water for a certain species of fish to swim by," she says.

Ian Frazier represents all the writers who inherit a vast hoard of family papers and mementos going back many generations and wonder how to even begin to weed it all out and shape it into a coherent story. Frazier started *Family* after his parents died within a year of each other, leaving an apartment in Ohio in which nothing had been thrown away. "Objects suggest narrative," Frazier says, and for two and a half years he dug like a paleontologist through his parents' hundreds of letters and artifacts — old neckties and purses and theater programs and Navy ID cards — to "infer the culture they came from and its plot" and thereby give meaning to their lives. He soon realized that their lives could only be given meaning within the context of the long decline of the Protestant establishment and its values. That gave him a second plot, intertwined with the first one, and deflected him down many overgrown trails of nineteenth-century American social history. "It's like building a house," he says. "You get to a certain part and you realize that you need a different gauge of lumber or something, and you have to go get it."

Henry Louis Gates, Jr., represents the writers who use memoir to record what it's like to belong to a minority culture in America. His *Colored People*, recalling his boyhood in Piedmont, West Virginia, written in a style suggestive of his father's storytelling voice, is pungently honest about how that black community went about its living and its loving. "I wanted to write a book that imitated the specialness of black culture when no white people are around," Gates says, noting that earlier black authors like Richard Wright and Ralph Ellison edited out of their work all such rollicking details that whites could use against their race. Such self-censorship is "totally bogus" to Gates. "If I had thought I was writing for middle-class ladies with white gloves on," he says, "I couldn't have written this book." His is the first generation of black males secure enough, he claims, to write a memoir without kowtowing to an imagined censor. He speaks for all ethnic Americans searching for their identity in a nation that becomes more balkanized every day. "If you ask me what the legacy of my book will be," Gates says, "I would like it to make younger people feel freer to tell their own stories."

Jill Ker Conway represents one of the most potent strains of memoir: growing up in a faraway place. In *The Road from Coorain* she vividly recalls her isolated girlhood on a sheep station in the Australian outback, the seven-year drought that killed her parents' homesteading dream and ended up killing her father, and the ordeal of separating herself from a suffocating male society and starting over in a new land. Hers is also a strongly feminist memoir. Conway describes how she rebelled against the "romantic plot" that women traditionally act out, acquiescing in seeing themselves as passive players in somebody else's story — even strong women like Conway's "great heroine," the reformer Jane Addams. "I thought it was important," she says, "to relate the story of a young woman taking charge of her own life in an unromantic way, in which it's perfectly clear that she arrives at a moment of choice."

So unassertive have women been about their identity, says Conway, who in her new life in America would become president of Smith College, that in this century eight autobiographies have been written by men for every one written by a woman. That kind of imbalance was one of my reasons for wanting Conway and Gates in this new edition of *Inventing the Truth*. Both of them write boldly about their escape from an unequal system. By that declaration of independence they empower everyone else who is disenfranchised or dislocated in the new America: women, minorities, immigrants and other social outsiders. Along with Eileen Simpson and Ian Frazier they join Russell Baker, Annie Dillard, Alfred Kazin, and Toni Morrison in shouting a loud message to all who embark on a memoir: Be true to yourself and to the culture that you were born into. Have the courage to tell your story as only you can tell it.

Two of the original talks, those of Russell Baker and Toni Morrison, are followed by excerpts from the question-and-answer period that led to further points about the writing process, and in the new chapters I've retained an occasional question of my own. Throughout, my aim was to preserve each writer's speaking voice. Listen, therefore, as you read. You'll hear eight writers talking about how they sorted out their memories and their emotions and arrived at a version of their past that they felt was true.

RUSSELL BAKER

Life with Mother

I'm primarily a journalist, a commercial writer, and I find it odd to be talking as a memoirist. Memoirs are for remembrance. And the remembrances of journalists, when they take book form, are what I think of as "and then I met" books. In my time as a journalist I have met many what we call great men — at least celebrated men. But in *Growing Up* I was not interested in doing an "and then I met" book. My prime interest was to celebrate people whom nobody had ever heard of. And whom I was terribly fond of, for the most part, and thought deserved to be known.

Why did I write this book? I asked my daughter the other day, "What should I say when I talk at the Public Library next week?" And she said, "You should say why you thought you had something so interesting to say that a large number of people would want to read it." And I said I hadn't anticipated that any number of people would want to read it; what I'd wanted was to write a book that I felt I had to write. It grew out of a number of things that had been happening in my life, perhaps starting at birth. As a writer I was blessed from the cradle, because I had the good fortune to be born into two very large, some people would say immense, families. The sort they don't make anymore.

My father was one of thirteen children, twelve of whom were boys. My mother was one of nine children, seven of whom were boys. So I came into the world well equipped with uncles. Twenty of them — that is, if you count my uncle Emil and my uncle Harold, who married Aunt Sally and Aunt Sister, respectively. What's more, a lot of these uncles got married, and this has provided me with a healthy supply of aunts. Now if you're destined to have a not very interesting life — and I was so destined — the next best thing, if you're going to be a writer, is to have a huge family. It gives you a chance to learn a lot about humanity from close-up observation.

I worry about people who get born nowadays, because they get born into such tiny families — sometimes into no family at all. When you're the only pea in the pod, your parents are likely to get you confused with the Hope Diamond. And that encourages you to talk too much. Getting into the habit of talking too much is fine if you're destined to be a lawyer or a politician or an entertainer. But if you're going to be a writer, it's death. We have many writers nowadays who don't realize this. Writers have to cultivate the habit early in life of listening to people other than themselves. And if you're born into a big family, as I was, you might as well learn to listen, because they're not going to give you much chance to talk. With twenty uncles and a dozen aunts, all old enough to have earned the right to speak whenever they wanted to open their mouths, there was not a great demand for us three children to put in our oar and to liven up the discussion.

I've never been able to complete an accurate count of the number of cousins I have. But I have cousins to the utmost degree. In addition to first cousins, I have second, third and fourth cousins, plus cousins many times removed. I have first cousins who are old enough to be my parents, and I have first cousins young enough to be my children. I'm constantly discovering cousins who were born when my attention was diverted somewhere else. Just recently I learned that the star of the Johns Hopkins lacrosse team is the great-grandson of my first cousin Myrtle, which I suppose makes him my great-grandcousin.

Now I cite these battalions of relatives not to boast about the fertility of my bloodline, but to illustrate why I spent most of my childhood learning to listen. When the grown-ups in a family that big said that children were born to be seen and not heard, they weren't just exercising the grown-up right to engage in picturesque speech and tired old maxims. Nor were they trying to stifle children's right to creative expression. For them holding down the uproar was a question of survival. And it was wonderful training if you are going to be a writer: having to give up the right to show off and be a childhood performer and just sit there, quietly watching and listening to the curious things grown-ups did and said.

Out of this experience, at least in my family, there grew a kind of home folklore tradition, which was sustained among those of us who had been children together — a habit of reminiscent storytelling, whenever we got together, about what we remembered from childhood. About the lives, deeds, sayings and wisdom of elders. About aunts, uncles, grandparents, great-aunts, strangers who would come courting, women who — as the phrase always went — put up with an awful lot.

Putting up with an awful lot was what women seemed to do in the days of my childhood. My cousin Lillian, who was nearly eighty when I interviewed her for *Growing Up* about my mother's relationship with my father, said, "Well, Russell, people said Betty was hard to get along with. But she had to put up with an awful lot." Indeed she did. I had my own stock of these family tales and was fond, when dining out and the wine was flowing a little too generously, of telling the company about the time my grandmother Baker scolded a visiting delegation of the Ku Klux Klan for making a mess of their mothers' bed sheets. Or the time the Jersey City cops arrested Uncle Jim for running a red light and took away his shoelaces so he wouldn't try to hang himself in the cell. With that many uncles you had a great variety of material.

My editor, Tom Congdon, was present at a few of these dinners when I was telling old stories, and after a while he began cajoling me to put them into some kind of book about what it was like growing up in an antique time in a big family. He began referring to it as "the growing up book." Of course I had no intention of writing it. I was already turning out a newspaper column three times a week, which meant grinding out a hundred thousand words a year for my job. Spending my leisure writing another couple of hundred thousand words was hardly my idea of amusement.

But long before Tom started stirring the creative waters, something had begun to bother me. To wit, middle age. My children arrived at adolescence in the 1960s — that slum of a decade — and the 1970s, not one of the vintage decades either. And I was dismayed to observe, as elderly folk usually do when the children hit adolescence, that the values I'd been bred to cherish and live by were now held in contempt by people of my children's age. What was even worse, those values were regarded as squalid — remnants of the despicable, social-political system that my generation had connived in creating for the suppression of freedom.

It seemed to me that these views came out of a profound ignorance of history. Not uncommon among adolescents. As I vaguely recalled from my own experience, adolescence was a time when you firmly believed that sex hadn't been invented until the year you started high school, when the very idea that anything interesting might have happened during your parents' lifetime was unthinkable. I knew because I had been an adolescent myself. I remembered how ludicrous I thought it was that anybody could have tolerated spending their youth in the dreary decades of Theodore Roosevelt, Woodrow Wilson and World War I, as my parents had.

With my children in this insufferable phase of life it became harder and harder to speak with them as a father ought to speak to his children. When I corrected them and undertook to advise them on how to do things right, I took my example from the way things were done in my days. Which produced a great deal of invisible but nevertheless palpable sneering. Adolescence was finishing its nasty work of turning them from dear sweet children into the same ornery people you meet every day as you go through life. The kind of people who insist on disagreeing with you. And behaving like people.

In the hope of breaking through that communications blackout I tried writing a few letters to them. Just a few. For I soon realized that these were the kind of letters that bore the eyes right out of an adolescent. They were long descriptions of my own childhood, in which I tried to convey to them some sense of how different and remote was the world that I had come from; to tell them about their own forebears, who had lived and died before they were born, so they might glean at least a hint that life was more than a single journey from the diaper to the shroud. I wanted my children to know that they were part of a long chain of humanity extending deep into the past and that they had some responsibility for extending it into the future.

Going through the carbons of some old correspondence recently, I was astonished to come across a couple of these letters that I had written the kids a long time ago and to recognize long blocks of writing that would appear again, not much changed, in *Growing Up*, which I wrote ten years later. And I realized that I'd been writing that book to my children long before Tom Congdon heard me writing it over the wine at dinner.

But what finally prompted the book to become a book was what I came to think of as the living death of my mother — whose mind went out one day as though every circuit in the city had been blown. I was in Key West at the time; my sister Doris called me and told me what had happened, and I flew up to Baltimore and went to the hospital — completely unprepared for what I was going to encounter. And I started talking to my mother, and she was completely gone. I was speechless. She was suffering from something that I have since come to recognize as very common to elderly folks but that I had never seen before and certainly had never thought would happen to my mother. I was so astonished that my only reaction was to start taking notes on what she was saying. I had stopped at the hospital gift shop, as people sometimes do, to take some knickknack up to her, not realizing what I was going to find, and I tore the paper bag open so that I could write on the back of it. And I started making a record of our conversation. It's a reporter's reflex. What I was hearing was so amazing that I instinctively began recording it on the back of this bag. When I left I stuffed it in a raincoat pocket and forgot about it. I found it many weeks later and put it in a desk drawer and again I forgot it for a long time. And that turned out to be the conversation that appears in the first chapter of *Growing Up* — that disjointed conversation.

When I realized what had happened to my mother I was in a kind of intellectual shock, and I didn't know how to deal with it for a long time. Gradually it seemed to me that the way to deal with it was to write about the times that the two of us had passed through together. And I began to do that. But being the good reporter, I had no concept of how to write a memoir. I knew nothing about it; I only knew how to report a magazine piece. So I took my tape recorder out and I interviewed many of my relatives, those who were still living — people in their eighties, one or two in their nineties — about the family, things I had never been interested in before. And my wife Mimi and I began doing the genealogy. Who were these people? I had no notion of who they were or where they had come from. And in the process I began to learn how interesting they were. They were people who would be extremely boring to read about in the newspaper, but they were fascinating. And I transcribed all these interviews and notes. I reported everything very carefully: a long piece of newspaper reportage. Then I started writing, and what I wrote was a reporter's book in which I quoted these elderly people talking about what life was like long ago in that time and place. I was reporting my own life and, being the good journalist, I kept myself out of it. And because I was uneasy about what had always been an awkward relationship with my mother and because she wasn't there to testify for herself, I kept *her* out of it. And I wrote a rather long book. I think it ran to four hundred and fifty pages in manuscript.

I was very pleased with it and I sent it off to my agent and my editor and I thought, "Well, I'll give them twenty-four hours to sit up all night and read it and they'll phone me back tomorrow." You always have that feeling of euphoria just about having finished anything. Well, there was no phone call the next day, nor the day after. Nobody called the next week, nor the week after that. A month passed and nobody called. By then Tom Congdon had his own publishing company, and I knew he was in financial trouble, and I told myself, "Tom is too busy trying to raise money to bother reading this great manuscript." And I put it in the drawer and forgot it.

Eventually I began to sense that there was something wrong, and one night I took it out of the drawer and sat down in my office and started to read. I nodded off on about page 20. And I thought, "If I can't read this thing . . ." But it was an intensely responsible book. Everything in it was correct, the quotations were accurate, everything had been double-checked. Finally, Tom, in despair, asked for a conference. Tom and I had worked together a long time, but he has never quite figured out how to tell me something is no good, and to tell somebody that a whole book is no good is tough for any editor, I guess.

But by that time I had made a second judgment myself that the book was in terrible shape and I knew what was wrong with it: My mother wasn't in it. There were all these interesting relatives, the uncles and the aunts and people talking from the present about the old days, but it was really nothing but journalism — reminiscences of today about yesterday. I had lunch with Tom and I said that I knew what was wrong with the book and that I would rewrite the whole thing. I said it was a book about a boy and his mother. It was about the tension between a child and his mother, and everything had to hinge on that. And Tom said he thought that was right — that I had made a grievous mistake in trying to write a book about myself in which I didn't appear. He didn't realize the strength of the mother character as I did, and I knew that if I brought the mother in and made her the hinge on which everything swung, the book would be a story. It would work as a book. I told Tom that's what I intended to do.

Now at one point Tom gave me a piece of advice, and I pass it on to any of you who are tempted someday to write your memoir. As I say, I had given Tom this manuscript of faithfully reported history of what people remembered of the '20s and '30s, and in it I had written what I thought was a good chapter about my uncle Harold. It's the one that begins: "Uncle Harold was famous for lying." And I knew that was a good chapter because I "got" Uncle Harold — I turned him into a character. I hadn't reported him; I made him the man whose memory lived inside me. At some point in the book I made a conclusion about him: I said that Uncle Harold, an uneducated and an unread man, was famous for being a great liar. But he wasn't really a liar; he just wanted life to be more interesting than it was. He lived a very dull life — he was a gravedigger at that time — and he liked to tell stories, but he didn't tell them very well. I said that in his primitive way Uncle Harold had perceived that the possibilities of achieving art lie not in reporting, but in fiction. And Tom Congdon sent that page back to me underlined in red, and he wrote on it, "I honor Uncle Harold."

Well, the problem that I knew, and that Tom didn't know at the time I resolved to rewrite the book, was that I had been dishonest about my mother. What I had written, though it was accurate to the extent that the reporting was there, was dishonest because of what I had left out. I had been unwilling to write honestly. And that dishonesty left a great hollow in the center of the original book.

Funny things happen to you when you really start to research something like this. I made a couple of serendipitous discoveries. One was that . . . well, my mother kept a trunk. I knew that. All good Southern ladies kept a trunk that they carried with them through life, and my mother was no exception. When she became incompetent, my sister took custody of this trunk, but my sister has no interest in that sort of thing, and she called my younger son, who was a pack rat, and told him to come over and take anything he was interested in out of it.

He was delighted. He went through the trunk and he came back with, among other things, a series of love letters that had been sent to my mother in the years 1932 and 1933, the depths of the Depression, by an immigrant Dane named Oluf. I had never known that she was in love with this man. It was obviously an unconsummated love affair because he was away most of the time. He moved to western Pennsylvania and they never saw each other after the most casual encounters.

Now I knew that what I was writing was a book about the Depression, and yet I dreaded having to write about it. Writing about the Depression is extremely dull — everybody knows the statistics, and I couldn't figure out any way to make this interesting. And yet the Depression was the very essence of the setting of this book. I kept worrying about how I was going to handle the Depression chapter. I made several passes at it, writing in terms of statistical reports. Then my son went through my mother's trunk and found Oluf's letters. They were almost illegible — he wrote in a fractured English that was hard to read, in a big flowing script, and there were many of these letters. I gave them to my wife. I said, "Read these and tell me if there's anything in them," and I went off to work. That evening when I got home she was visibly moved. She said, "This is the story of a man who was destroyed by the Depression."

So I read them, and it was the most moving story. It was a self-contained story. And while I was moved, I was also delighted, because it had solved my Depression problem. Here was what the Depression meant to one man. That made a chapter which cleared up a lot of problems and some mysteries about my mother.

The second serendipitous discovery that came from that trunk was my mother's marriage certificate, which my son brought me in Nantucket. He paid me a surprise call. One summer day I was sitting in the backyard sunning myself, and my son came in the yard grinning. "You won't guess what I've got," he said. It was my mother's marriage certificate. And I looked at it: She was married in March of the year in which I was born in August. I was fifty-four years old and I realized I was a love child.

Well, it made me feel a little more interesting than I was. And it also cleared up a number of things — mysteries that I hadn't been able to solve in the first version of the book. Why my mother and my grandmother (my father's mother) detested each other so deeply. Why my mother left that part of the world so rapidly after my father died. The morning she learned that he was dead, she called her brother in New Jersey and announced that she was going to come live with him.

All of these things that had left me utterly baffled suddenly fell into place. And then I realized, too, why she had opposed so deeply my own relationship with the woman who was ultimately to be my wife. Everything fell into place, made a story. The question was, Could I write this? I hadn't written it in the book, and it made that first book a lie. So, in revising, I determined I would write that story. I thought, "If I want to honor my mother in this book I must be truthful." But I did it with great trepidation. Because you could be accused of vulgarity, of airing dirty linen and exploiting your dying mother for commercial purposes. And yet I felt that it dishonored her to lie about it.

So I decided to do it. I decided that although nobody's life makes any sense, if you're going to make a book out of it you might as well make it into a story. I remember saying to my wife, "I am now going upstairs to invent the story of my life." And I started writing, on the days when I wasn't doing my column, and I rewrote that whole book — almost the entire thing, with the exception of a couple of chapters — in about six months. That was the book that was eventually published.

But first I took the manuscript to my sister Doris — the two of us had grown up together — and had her read it. I anticipated that she was going to raise violent objections to my mentioning the fact that my mother had been pregnant before her marriage. And she did object, but not violently. Rationally, she said she thought that was a disgraceful thing to publish about Mother. And I told her pretty much what I've just told you: that I thought honesty would serve my mother best in the long run; it would make her plausible in this book, in which she might live

longer than most of us if it worked right. And that anyhow, nowadays, nobody cared. "So be it," said Doris, and we
published.

Still, I was very worried about the public reaction. God
knows what was going to happen about that. I worried
about that more than about anything else in the book. And
I remember being deeply moved the day the *Wall Street
Journal* ran its review, which was by Michael Gartner. The
first sentence began: "Russell Baker's mother, a miracu-
lous woman . . ."

*

Q. What were the reactions of your children?

I don't know. Although we are very close to our children, there are certain things children don't tell their parents. The children liked the book, surely. And they were
proud of it, I think. My daughter, our oldest, said she was
grateful for the book because it gave her her grandmother,
whom she had only known when she was a baby.

Q. How much of your book is truthful and how much is
good writing?

Well, all the incidents are truthful. A book like that has
certain things in common with fiction. Anything that is
autobiographical is the opposite of biography. The biographer's problem is that he never knows enough. The
autobiographer's problem is that he knows much too much.
He knows absolutely everything; he knows the whole iceberg, not just the tip. I mean, Henry James knew all the
things that have puzzled Leon Edel for years; he knew
what that tragic moment was that happened. So when

you're writing about yourself, the problem is what to leave out. And I just left out almost everything — there's only about half a percent in that book. You wouldn't want everything; it would be like reading the *Congressional Record*. But the incidents that *are* in the book, of course they happened.

For example, there's a long account of the day of my father's death, which occurred when I was five. People said, "How could you have known that?" I knew that. That was the first thing I knew. That whole day began to happen as if I was sitting in the theater of life and the curtain was going up. It was the start of my life. I can still hear people talking that day. I know what the air smelled like. I know what people's faces looked like. How they were dressed. What they were eating. Don't ask me what I did yesterday — I'd have to look in my diary — but that I knew. I didn't do anything in the book that wasn't right.

Q. How did you decide what to put in and what to leave out?

I decided that the story line was the mother and the son: this extremely strong woman and weak male. There are three strong women in the book — the grandmother, the mother and the woman that the son marries at the end — and it's the story of the tension that these various women put on each other and on the male figure. I don't have a lot in the book that doesn't contribute to that point of view of what the story material was.

Q. I wanted to ask you about another woman in the book that I found unforgettable: your wife. Was she in the first version as she was in the book that I read?

She didn't appear in the first version. Because of the business about my mother and my birth, I didn't need Mimi. I didn't want to go that far. But I finally saw that to make the book an integral work I needed her — she was the logical completion of the series of events that started with my birth. I hated to use the material because it was material for another book that I'd often thought of writing. And I threw it away in ten or fifteen thousand words.

Mimi was a good sport, though. When I told her that I thought the book needed this, she was very supportive. I said, "Do you mind if I write about it?" and she said, "No, go ahead." And I interviewed her just the way I did everybody else. She was a terrible interview. She lied like a politician. But I interviewed her and I went up and wrote those concluding chapters. They went very quickly. And I brought it to her finally and said, "Read through it, and if there's anything you want cut, I'll cut it." Well, after reading it she said she thought I had left out certain events that would make it more interesting. I was sort of shocked at some of the things she suggested ought to be added, and I said, "Look, I'm a writer who's used to dealing with sensitive material — let me make the decision." And my decision was not to add a thing.

Well, after several months we got the first copies of the book in the mail, and Mimi immediately grabbed one, took it to the bedroom, closed the door and read all afternoon. When she came out she looked appalled. "Well, what do you think?" I said to her, and she said, "It looks different in print."

"That's what they always say," I told her.

ANNIE DILLARD

To Fashion a Text

I'm here because I'm writing a book called *An American Childhood*, which is a memoir — insofar as a memoir is any account, usually in the first person, of incidents that happened a while ago. It isn't an autobiography, and it isn't "memoirs." I wouldn't dream of writing my memoirs; I'm only forty years old. Or my autobiography; any chronology of my days would make very dull reading — I've spent about thirty years behind either a book or a desk. The book that I'm writing is an account of a childhood in Pittsburgh, Pennsylvania, where I grew up.

The best memoirs, I think, forge their own forms. The writer of any work, and particularly any nonfiction work, must decide two crucial points: what to put in and what to leave out.

So I thought, "What shall I put in?" Well, what is the book about? *An American Childhood* is about the passion of childhood. It's about a child's vigor, and originality, and eagerness, and mastery, and joy.

It's about waking up. A child wakes up over and over again, and notices that she's living. She dreams along, loving the exuberant life of the senses, in love with beauty and power, oblivious of herself, and then suddenly, bingo, she wakes up and feels herself alive. She notices her own awareness. And she notices that she is set down here, mysteriously, in a going world. The world is full of fascinating information that she can collect and enjoy. And the world is public; its issues are moral and historical ones.

So the book is about two things: a child's interior life — vivid, superstitious and timeless — and a child's growing awareness of the world. The structural motion of the book is from the interior landscape — one brain's own idiosyncratic topography — to the American landscape, the vast setting of our common history. The little child pinches the skin on the back of her hand and sees where God made Adam from spit and clay. The older child explores the city on foot and starts to work on her future as a detective, or an epidemiologist, or a painter. Older yet, she runs wild and restless over the city's bridges, and finds in Old Testament poetry and French symbolist poetry some language sounds she loves.

The interior life is in constant vertical motion; consciousness runs up and down the scales every hour like a slide trombone. It dreams down below; it notices up above; and it notices itself, too, and its own alertness. The vertical motion of consciousness, from inside to outside and back, interests me. I've written about it once before, in an essay about a solar eclipse, and I wanted to do more with it.

For a private interior life, I've picked — almost at random — my own. As an aside, this isn't as evident as it may seem. I simply like to write books. About twelve years ago, while I was walking in Acadia National Park in Maine, I decided to write a narrative — a prose narrative, because I wanted to write prose. After a week's thought I decided to write mostly about nature, because I thought I could make it do what I wanted, and I decided to set it all on the coast of Maine. I decided further to write it in the third person, about a man, a sort of metaphysician, in his fifties. A month or so later I decided reluctantly to set the whole shebang in Virginia, because I knew more about Virginia. Then I decided to write it in the first person, as a man. Not until I had written the first chapter and showed it around — this was *Pilgrim at Tinker Creek* — did I give up the pretext of writing in the first person as a man. I wasn't out to deceive people; I just didn't like the idea of writing about myself. I knew I wasn't the subject.

So in this book, for simplicity's sake, I've got my own interior life. It was a lively one. I put in what it was that had me so excited all the time — the sensation of time pelting me as if I were standing under a waterfall. I loved the power of the life in which I found myself. I loved to feel its many things in all their force. I put in what it feels like to play with the skin on your mother's knuckles. I put in what it feels like to throw a baseball — you aim your whole body at the target and watch the ball fly off as if it were your own head. I put in drawing pencil studies of my baseball mitt and collecting insects and fooling around with a microscope.

In my study on Cape Cod, where I write, I've stuck above my desk a big photograph of a little Amazonian boy whose face is sticking out of a waterfall or a rapids. White water is pounding all around his head, in a kind of wreath, but his face is absolutely still, looking up, and his black eyes are open dreamily on the distance. That little boy is completely alive; he's letting the mystery of existence beat on him. He's having his childhood, and I think he knows it. And I think he will come out of the water strong, and ready to do some good. I see this photograph whenever I look up from my computer screen.

So I put in that moment of waking up and noticing that you've been put down in a world that's already under way. The rushing of time wakes you: You play along mindless and eternal on the kitchen floor, and time streams in full flood beside you on the floor. It rages beside you, down its swollen banks, and when it wakes you you're so startled you fall in.

When you wake up, you notice that you're here.

"Here," in my case, was Pittsburgh. I put in the three rivers that meet here. The Allegheny from the north and the Monongahela from the south converge to form the Ohio, the major tributary of the Mississippi, which, in turn, drains the whole continent east of the divide via the Missouri River rising in the Rocky Mountains. The great chain of the Alleghenies kept pioneers out of Pittsburgh

until the 1760s, one hundred and fifty years after James-
town.

I put in those forested mountains and hills, and the way
the three rivers lie flat and moving among them, and the
way the low land lies wooded among them, and the way
the blunt mountains rise in the darkness from the rivers'
banks.

I put in Lake Erie, and summers along its mild shore. I
put in New Orleans, the home of Dixieland jazz, where
my father was heading when he jumped in his boat one
day to go down the river like Huck Finn.

I put in the pioneers who "broke wilderness," and the
romance of the French and Indian Wars that centered
around Fort Duquesne and Fort Pitt. I put in the brawling
rivermen — the flatboatmen and keelboatmen. I put in
the old Scotch-Irish families who dominate Pittsburgh
and always have. The Mellons are Scotch-Irish, and so
were Andrew Carnegie and Henry Clay Frick. They're all
Presbyterians. I grew up in this world, at the lunatic fringe
of it, and it fascinates me. I think it's important. I think it's
peculiarly American — that mixture of piety and acquisi-
tiveness, that love of work. They're Calvinists, of course
— just like the Massachusetts Puritans — and I think I
can make a case that their influence on American thought
was greater than the Puritans'. There were far more
Scotch-Irish Presbyterians, after all, and they settled all
over the American colonies and carried their democracy
and pragmatism with them.

In Pittsburgh the Scotch-Irish constitute a world of
many families whose forebears knew each other, who re-

spect each other's discretion and who admire each other for occupying their slots without fuss. The men are withdrawn, the women are ironic. They believe in their world; they all stay in Pittsburgh, and their children stay there. I alone am escaped to tell thee. I and David McCullough, who grew up a few houses away. And James Laughlin, the publisher. All of us Pittsburgh Scotch-Irish Presbyterians.

My sisters and I grew up in this world, and I put it in *An American Childhood*. I put in our private school and quiet club and hushed neighborhood where the houses were stone and their roofs were slate. I put in dancing with little boys at dancing school, and looking at the backs of their interesting necks at Presbyterian church.

Just to make trouble, I put in money. My grandmother used to tell me never to touch money with my bare hands.

I put in books, for that's where this book started, with an essay I wrote for the *New York Times Magazine* on reading books. Almost all of my many passionate interests, and my many changes of mind, came through books. Books prompted the many vows I made to myself. Nonfiction books lured me away from the world — as I dreamed about working for Scotland Yard, doing field work in freshwater streams, rock collecting in the salt desert, painting in Paris. And novels dragged me back into the world — because I would read whatever was handy, and what was handy in those years were novels about the Second World War. I read so many books about the Second World War that I knew how to man a minesweeper before I knew how to walk in high heels. You couldn't read much about the war without figuring out that the world was a moral arena that required your strength.

I had the notion back then that everything was interesting if you just learned enough about it. Now, writing about it, I have the pleasure of learning it all again and finding that it *is* interesting. I get to inform myself and any readers about such esoterica as rock collecting, which I hadn't thought about in almost thirty years.

When I was twelve a paperboy gave me two grocery bags full of rock and mineral chunks. It took me most of a year to identify them. At a museum shop I bought cards of what they called thumbnail specimens. And I read books about a fairly absurd batch of people who called themselves rockhounds; they spent their evenings in the basement sawing up slabs of travertine into wavy slices suitable, they said, for wall hangings.

Now, in this memoir, I get to recall where the romance of rock collecting had lain: the symbolic sense that underneath the dreary highways, underneath Pittsburgh, were canyons of crystals — that you could find treasure by prying open the landscape. In my reading I learned that people have cracked knobs of granite and laid bare clusters of red garnets and topaz crystals, chrysoberyl, spudomene and emerald. They held in their hands crystals that had hung in a hole in the dark for a billion years unseen. I liked the idea of that. I would lay about me right and left with a hammer and bash the landscape to bits. I would crack the earth's crust like a piñata and spread its vivid prizes in chunks to the light. That's what I wanted to do. So I put that in.

It's also a great pleasure to write about my parents, because they're both great storytellers — comedians, actually — which gives me a chance to tell their wonderful stories. We were all young, at our house, and we enjoyed ourselves.

My father was a dreamer; he lived differently from other men around him. One day he abruptly quit the family firm, when I was ten, and took off down the Ohio River in a boat by himself to search out the roots of jazz in New Orleans. He came back after several months and withdrew from corporate life forever. He knew the world well — all sort of things, which he taught us to take an interest in: how people build bridge pilings in the middle of a river, how jazz came up the river to be educated in Chicago, how the pioneers made their way westward from Pittsburgh, down the Ohio River, sitting on the tops of their barges and singing "Bang Away, My Lulu."

My mother was both a thinker and what one might call a card. If she lay on the beach with friends and found the conversation dull, she would give a little push with her heel and roll away. People were stunned. She rolled deadpan and apparently effortlessly, her arms and legs extended tidily, down the beach to the distant water's edge, where she lay at ease just as she had been, but half in the surf, and well out of earshot. She was not only a card but a wild card, a force for disorder. She regarded even tiny babies as straight men, and liked to step on the drawstring of a crawling baby's gown, so that the baby crawled and crawled and never got anywhere except into a little ball at the top of the gown.

She was interested in language. Once my father and I were in the kitchen listening to a ballgame — the Pirates playing the New York Giants. The Giants had a utility infielder named Wayne Terwilliger. Just as Mother walked through the kitchen, the announcer said, "Terwilliger bunts one." Mother stopped dead and said, "What was that? Was that English?" Father said, "The man's name is Terwilliger. He bunted." Mother thought that was terrific. For the next ten or twelve years she made this surprising string of syllables her own. If she was testing a microphone, or if she was pretending to whisper a secret in my ear, she said, "Terwilliger bunts one." If she had ever had an occasion to create a motto for a coat of arms, as Andrew Carnegie had, her motto would have been "Terwilliger bunts one." Carnegie's was "Death to privilege."

These fine parents taught my sisters and me moral courage, insofar as we have it, and tolerance, and how to dance all night without dragging your arms on your partner, and how to time the telling of a joke.

I've learned a lot by writing this book, not only about writing but about American history. Eastern woodland Indians killed many more settlers than plains Indians did. By the time settlers made it to Sioux and Apache country those Indians had been so weakened by disease and by battles with the army that they didn't have much fight left in them. It was the settlers in the Pennsylvania forests and in Maryland and Virginia who kept getting massacred and burned out and taken captive and tortured. During the four years the French held Pittsburgh at Fort Duquesne they armed the Indians and sent them out from there, raiding and killing English-speaking settlers. These were mostly Scotch-Irish, because the Penn family let them settle in Pennsylvania only if they would serve as a "buffer sect" between Quakers and Indians. When the English held Pittsburgh at Fort Pitt they gave the Indians unwashed blankets from the smallpox hospital.

I put in early industry, because it was unexpectedly interesting. Before there was steel, everything was made out of wrought iron — which I find just amazing. Railroad ties were made out of wrought iron, as if they were candle sconces. Men had to carry wrought iron railroad ties all up and down the country. Wrought iron is made by iron puddlers, who belong to the iron puddlers' union, the Sons of Vulcan. It's a very difficult process: you stir slag back into iron, and it requires skilled labor because carbon monoxide bubbles up. The language is also nice. To sinter, for instance, is to convert flu dust to clinker. And I finally learned what coke is. When I was a child I thought that Coca-Cola was a by-product of steelmaking.

I learned about the heyday of the big industrialists and the endless paradox of Andrew Carnegie, the only one of the great American moguls who not only read books but actually wrote them, including one with a very American title, *The Gospel of Wealth*. He sold U.S. Steel to J. P. Morgan for $492 million, and he said, "A man who dies rich dies disgraced." He gave away ninety percent of his fortune in the few years he had left. While he was giving away money, many people were moved, understandably, to write him letters. He got one such letter from his friend Mark Twain. It said:

You seem to be in prosperity. Could you lend an admirer a dollar & a half to buy a hymn-book with? God will bless you. I feel it. I know it.
P.S. Don't send the hymn-book, send the money.

Carnegie was only five feet three inches tall. He weighed 133 pounds. He built the workers free libraries and museums and an art gallery at the same time that he had them working sixteen hours a day, six days a week, at subhuman wages, and drinking water full of typhoid and cholera because he and the other business owners opposed municipal works like water filtration plants. By 1906 Pittsburgh had the highest death rate in the nation because of wretched living conditions, and yet it was the seat of "wealth beyond computation, wealth beyond imagination." People built stables for their horses with gold mirrors in the stalls. The old Scotch-Irish families were horrified at the new millionaires who popped up around this time because they liked things pretty quiet. One new millionaire went to a barber on Penn Avenue for his first shampoo and the barber reported that the washing brought out "two ounces of fine Mesabi ore and a scattering of slag and cinders."

And what to leave out?
Well, I'm not writing social history. This is not one of those books in which you may read the lyrics or even the

titles of popular songs on the radio. Or the names of radio and TV programs, or advertising slogans or product names or clothing fashions. I don't like all that. I want to direct the reader's attention in equal parts to the text — as a formal object — and to the world, as an interesting place in which we find ourselves.

So another thing I left out, as far as I could, was myself. The personal pronoun can be the subject of the verb: "I see this, I did that." But not the object of the verb: "I analyze me, I discuss me, I describe me, I quote me."

In the course of writing this memoir I've learned all sorts of things, quite inadvertently, about myself and various relationships. But these things are not important to the book and I easily leave them out. Since the subject of the book is not me, other omissions naturally follow. I leave out many things that were important to my life but of no concern for the present book, like the summer I spent in Wyoming when I was fifteen. I keep the action in Pittsburgh; I see no reason to drag everybody off to Wyoming just because I want to tell them about my summer vacation. You have to take pains in a memoir not to hang on the reader's arm, like a drunk, and say, "And then I did this and it was so interesting." I don't write for that reason.

On the other hand, I dig deeply into the exuberant heart of a child and the restless, violent heart of an adolescent — and I was that child and I was that adolescent.

I leave out my private involvement with various young men. I didn't want to kiss and tell. I did put in several sections, however, about boys in general and the fascination they exerted. I ran around with one crowd of older boys so decadent, so accustomed to the most glittering of social lives, that one of them carried with him at all times, in his jacket pocket, a canister of dance wax so that he could be ready for anything. Other boys carry Swiss Army knives for those occasions which occur unexpectedly; this boy carried dance wax for the same reason. He could just sprinkle it on the dining room floor and take you in his arms and whirl you away. These were the sort of boys I knew; they had worn ties from the moment their mothers could locate their necks.

I tried to leave out anything that might trouble my family. My parents are quite young. My sisters are watching this book carefully. Everybody I'm writing about is alive and well, in full possession of his faculties, and possibly willing to sue. Things were simpler when I wrote about muskrats.

Writing in the first person can trap the writer into airing grievances. When I taught writing I spent a lot of time trying to convince young writers that, while literature is an art, it's not a martial art — that the pages of a short story or a novel are no place to defend yourself from an attack, real or imagined, and no place from which to launch an attack, particularly an attack against the very people who painstakingly reared you to your present omniscience.

I have no temptation to air grievances; in fact, I have no grievances left. Unfortunately, I seem to have written the story of my impassioned adolescence so convincingly that my parents (after reading that section of my book) think I still feel that way. It's a problem that I have to solve — one of many in this delicate area. My parents and my youngest sister still live in Pittsburgh; I have to handle it with tongs.

As a result of all of this, I've promised my family that each may pass on the book. I've promised to take out anything that anyone objects to — anything at all. When I was growing up I didn't really take to Pittsburgh society, and I was happy to throw myself into any other world I could find. But I guess I can't say so, because my family may think that I confuse them with conventional Pittsburgh society people in the '50s.

I know a writer who cruelly sticks his parents into all his short stories and still pleases them both, because his mother is pleased to see his father look bad and his father is pleased to see his mother look bad. I had, I thought, nothing but good to say about all named people, but I'll make all that better yet. I don't believe in a writer's kicking around people who don't have access to a printing press. They can't defend themselves.

My advice to memoir writers is to embark upon a memoir for the same reason that you would embark on any other book: to fashion a text. Don't hope in a memoir to preserve your memories. If you prize your memories as they are, by all means avoid — eschew — writing a memoir. Because it is a certain way to lose them. You can't put together a memoir without cannibalizing your own life for parts. The work battens on your memories. And it replaces them.

It's a matter of writing's vividness for the writer. If you

spend a couple of days writing a tricky paragraph, and if you spend a week or two laying out a scene or describing an event, you've spent more time writing about it than you did living it. The writing time is also much more intense.

After you've written, you can no longer remember anything but the writing. However true you make that writing, you've created a monster. This has happened to me many, many times, because I'm willing to turn events into pieces of paper. After I've written about any experience, my memories — those elusive, fragmentary patches of color and feeling — are gone; they've been replaced by the work. The work is a sort of changeling on the doorstep — not your baby but someone else's baby rather like it, different in some way that you can't pinpoint, and yours has vanished.

Memory is insubstantial. Things keep replacing it. Your batch of snapshots will both fix and ruin your memory of your travels, or your childhood, or your children's childhood. You can't remember anything from your trip except this wretched collection of snapshots. The painting you did of the light on the water will forever alter the way you see the light on the water; so will looking at Flemish paintings. If you describe a dream you'll notice that at the end of the verbal description you've lost the dream but gained a verbal description. You have to like verbal descriptions a lot to keep up this sort of thing. I like verbal descriptions a lot.

Let me put in a word now for a misunderstood genre: literary nonfiction. It's interesting to me because I try to write it and because I respect the art of it very much.

I like to be aware of a book as a piece of writing, and aware of its structure as a product of mind, and yet I want to be able to see the represented world through it. I admire artists who succeed in dividing my attention more or less evenly between the world of their books and the art of their books. In fiction we might say that the masters are Henry James and Herman Melville. In nonfiction the writer usually just points to the world and says, "This is a biography of Abraham Lincoln. This is what Abraham Lincoln was about." But the writer may also make of his work an original object in its own right, so that a reader may study the work with pleasure as well as the world that it describes. That is, works of nonfiction can be coherent and crafted works of literature.

It's not simply that they're carefully written, or vivid and serious and pleasing, like Boswell's *Life of Johnson*, say, or St.-Exupéry's wonderful memoir of early aviation, *Wind, Sand, and Stars*. It's not even that they may contain elements of fiction, that their action reveals itself in scenes that use visual descriptions and that often use dialogue. It's not just these things, although these things are important. It's that nonfiction accounts may be literary insofar as the parts of their structures cohere internally, insofar as the things are in them for the sake of the work itself, and insofar as the work itself exists in the service of idea. (It is especially helpful if the writer so fully expresses the idea in materials that only a trained technician can find it. Because the abstract structure of a given text, which is of great interest to the writer and serves to rouse him out of bed in the morning and impel him to the desk, is of little or no interest to the reader, and he'd better not forget it.)

Nonfiction accounts don't ordinarily meet these criteria, but they may. Walden Pond is the linchpin of a metaphysic. In repeated and self-conscious rewritings Thoreau hammered at its unremarkable and rather dreary acres until they fastened eternity in time and stood for the notion that the physical world itself expresses a metaphysical one. He picked up that pond and ran with it. He could just as readily have used something else — a friend, say, or a chestnut. You can do quite a bit with language.

Hemingway in *Green Hills of Africa* wrote a sober narrative account of killing a kudu, the whole of which functions as an elaborate metaphor for internal quests and conquests. Loren Eiseley lays in narrative symbols with a trowel, splashing mortar all over the place, but they hold. In his essay "The Star-Thrower," Eiseley's beachcomber who throws dying starfish back into the surf stands for any hope or mercy that flies in the face of harsh natural law. He stands finally for the extravagant spirit behind creation as a whole; he is a god hurling solar systems into the void.

I only want to remind my writing colleagues that a great deal can be done in nonfiction, especially in first-person accounts where the writer controls the materials absolutely. Because other literary genres are shrinking. Poetry has purified itself right out of the ballpark. Literary fiction is scarcely being published — it's getting to be like conceptual art. All that the unknown writer of fiction can do is to tell his friends about the book he has written, and all that his friends can say is "Good idea." The short story is to some extent going the way of poetry, limiting its subject matter to such narrow surfaces that it can't handle the things that most engage our hearts and minds. But literary nonfiction is all over the map and has been for three hundred years. There's nothing you can't do with it. No subject matter is forbidden, no structure is proscribed. You get to make up your own form every time.

When I gave up writing poetry I was very sad, for I had devoted fifteen years to the study of how the structures of poems carry meaning. But I was delighted to find that nonfiction prose can also carry meaning in its structures and, like poetry, can tolerate all sorts of figurative language, as well as alliteration and even rhyme. The range of rhythms in prose is larger and grander than it is in poetry, and it can handle discursive ideas and plain information as well as character and story. It can do everything. I felt as though I had switched from a single reed instrument to a full orchestra.

Let me close with a word about process. There's a common notion that self-discipline is a freakish peculiarity of writers — that writers differ from other people by possessing enormous and equal portions of talent and willpower. They grit their powerful teeth and go into their little rooms. I think that's a bad misunderstanding of what impels the writer. What impels the writer is a deep love for and respect for language, for literary forms, for books. It's a privilege to muck about in sentences all morning. It's a challenge to bring off a powerful effect, or to tell the truth about something. You don't do it from willpower; you do it from an abiding passion for the field. I'm sure it's the same in every other field.

Writing a book is like rearing children — willpower has very little to do with it. If you have a little baby crying in the middle of the night, and if you depend only on will-power to get you out of bed to feed the baby, that baby will starve. You do it out of love. Willpower is a weak idea; love is strong. You don't have to scourge yourself with a cat-o'-nine-tails to go to the baby. You go to the baby out of love for that particular baby. That's the same way you go to your desk. There's nothing freakish about it. Caring passionately about something isn't against nature, and it isn't against human nature. It's what we're here to do.

ALFRED KAZIN

The Past Breaks Out

A Walker in the City, published in 1951 as a sensory memory of boyhood in the Brownsville district of Brooklyn, began as something else. When the war, Hitler's war, was over, I returned from wartime reporting in England to find that there was no room for me in New York except in a ramshackle painter's studio on Pineapple Street in Brooklyn Heights, indifferently left to me when the painter moved on to big money in commercial art. He even left me his old paintings, which consisted of violently colored images, a whole series of concentration camp prisoners standing with clenched fists behind barbed wire.

The house itself had seen better days. The greasy, spattered front steps, just off the Chinese hand laundry in the basement, led into what must have been the vestibule of a traditionally stately Brooklyn Heights mansion. Despite the metal shields holding up the battered front door, you could see that it had once been a beautiful door, like the many beautiful doors of grand old brownstones still lining Columbia Heights, Hicks Street and the other streets veering toward the harbor and Brooklyn Bridge.

Pineapple Street, just off Fulton, was in a poor way just then, and so was I. Across the street, just above the garbage cans put out by the local coffeeshop, hung the lopsided bronze plaque put up by the Authors League commemorating the exact site where in 1851 Walt Whitman himself helped put *Leaves of Grass* into type. Whenever I went up to my top floor studio I could smell the remains of some ancient smoke. There had once been a fire. The building still smelled of fire. My two rooms on the top floor had obviously been cut out of something larger, and despite the makeshift wall between the Puerto Rican carpenter next door and myself, he woke me every morning when Pineapple Street was still dark just by the racket he made on the other side of the wall getting himself ready to leave for work.

I would lie in bed listening to tugs hooting three blocks away; the harbor was all around me, and, when it rained, my painter's great north windows were awash with foggy sea light. The floors went every which way, but there was a skylight; the place was full of light. The evenings were lonely and even a little terrible as I lay on a couch in the other room staring at the violently colored concentration camp prisoners, grim behind barbed wire. I had no respect for these paintings, but would not take them down.

Much as I had always loved the neighboring streets and walking the promenade below Columbia Heights, with its full view of *the* bridge of bridges and the port of New York,

I was unsure of everything else. A moment had come into my life, as can happen to men after thirty, when only the opening of Dante's *Inferno* spoke to my condition: "In the middle of our life, I found myself in a dark wood, for the straight way was lost."

A marriage had broken down during the war; I had not recovered. Hitler and his war had come to an end; it would never be over for me. On April 15, 1945, when I was still reporting political discussion groups in the British Army, a British detachment in the north of Germany had stumbled on the deeply hidden Belsen concentration camp in the vicinity of Hanover to find typhus raging, forty thousand sick, starving, dying prisoners, thirteen thousand corpses stacked on the ground. The London *Times* carried a dispatch from a correspondent with the army unit: "I have something to report that lies beyond the imagination of mankind." A week or so later, waiting out in the rain in the entrance to a music store, I heard a radio playing into the street the first Sabbath service from Belsen. When the liberated Jewish prisoners in unison recited the *Shema* — "Hear, O Israel, the Lord Our God, the Lord Is One" — I felt myself carried back to the old Friday evenings at home, when with the Sabbath at sundown a healing quietness would come over Brownsville.

In Pineapple Street, surrounded by New York and the harbor through which my parents as young rebels still unknown to each other had entered the country, I dreamed of putting my life in order by writing a book set against the New York background. This was no great departure from the criticism I had been writing for years. Criticism for me was not a theory, least of all a theory holding academics together. It was a branch of literature, a way of writing like any other — of characterization, analysis and almost physical empathy. Far from feeling confined to one mode of writing, I had been keeping all my life, since boyhood, a voluminous daily journal, or sketchbook, into which went everything that I felt like describing and thinking about.

What I liked most about this intimate record was writing in it, first thing every morning, in complete spontaneity and naturalness, lifelike and at the quick, as the French say. It represented some effort to think my life out. It also got me away from editors and their subjective dogmas about the public taste and capacity; this, at least, was all for myself. At the same time it was a cherished connection with something fundamental to American literature — the writing of personal history: diaries, journals, letters, memoirs. The influence of Puritanism had created a habit of mind that had persisted into the "American Renaissance" and the peculiarly personal reverberations in Emerson, Thoreau, Whitman and how many others — the need to present to God, the Eternal Reader and Judge of the soul's pilgrimage on earth, the veritable record of one's inner life.

At fourteen or fifteen my fascination with autobiography as narrative had accelerated when *The Education of Henry Adams* went on sale at the Abraham and Straus department store on Fulton Street in downtown Brooklyn. Without being able to say why, I knew that this particular book was more for me than the other book on sale, *The Autobiography of Benvenuto Cellini.*

There was something odd and even comic about what was to develop into a lifelong passion for everything to do with the Adamses. I was the first native child of Russian Jews, lived in the mostly Jewish (now mostly black) Brownsville district near the end of the I.R.T. subway, a notoriously rough, tough neighborhood trailing out into haunts of the Mafia. If my mother had known the sour opinions of Jews developed by the violently disillusioned patrician Henry Adams, the grandson and great-grandson of presidents, the most brilliant descendant of the most gifted American political family, she would have thrown *The Education of Henry Adams* out of the house — and me right after it.

But my mother didn't read English; she didn't read anything. It might have been interesting to inform my mother that Henry Adams's great-grandmother Abigail had written to her husband John during the Battle of Bunker Hill, "The race is not to the swift, nor the battle to the strong, but the God of Israel is He that giveth strength and power unto His people. Trust in Him at all times, ye people pour out your hearts before Him. God is a refuge for me — Charlestown is laid in ashes." After the Civil War, when the race *was* to the swift, Henry Adams felt himself so out of it that he likened himself to a Jew. "Had he been born in Jerusalem under the shadow of the Temple, and circumcised in the Synagogue by his uncle the high priest, under the name of Israel Cohen, he would scarcely have been more distinctly branded, and not much more heavily handicapped in the races of the coming century."

There was never a chance to go into such interesting

items of American history with my mother — to explain why Henry Adams so came to associate capitalism with Jews that he habitually referred to J. P. Morgan as a Jew. My mother lived apart from such intellectual hatreds. She had come to America as a young seamstress because she believed herself to be unmarriageable, a plain girl in a family where a good-looking sister, named Shana ("Beautiful"), was the favorite. To remain unmarried was unthinkable for a good Jewish girl.

In America my mother found my father-to-be. That, so to speak, was the limit of her acquaintance with the country. But getting to America did save my mother's life; Shana and her husband were to be horribly killed by the Nazis in a roundup of their village. In any event, my mother's America, though not extensive, was certainly intense. It consisted of her family alive in America, dead or dying in Russia, and the sewing machine in our kitchen, where as a "home" dressmaker she kept my sister and me in college during the Depression when my father, a housepainter, could find occasional day jobs only when the New Deal shelled out for the painting of subway stations and bridges.

My debt to *The Education of Henry Adams* and other "personal" American classics — the essays and journals of Emerson; *Walden* and the journals of Thoreau especially; *Leaves of Grass* and Whitman's diary of the Civil War, *Specimen Days* — is simply stated. One could be a writer without writing a novel. Every taxi driver and bartender who told you his story wanted to be a novelist. It was the expected, the Big Thing, in America especially; it had raised to the heights literary prima donnas from Mark Twain to Norman Mailer. It seemed positively perverse to Leslie Fiedler, when he reviewed my *A Walker in the City*, that the book "obstinately refuses to become a novel."

At the moment, however, waking up uneasily every morning in Pineapple Street to the glare of postwar New York, so different from the Depression '30s and my early working-class life in Brownsville, I was trying to write something about the city at large that would do justice to the color, the variety, the imperial range I encountered walking about the city every day. Every next day I tried to get into my notebook what Whitman in his greatest New York poem, "Crossing Brooklyn Ferry," had called "the glories strung like beads on my smallest sights and hearings — on the walk in the street, and the passage over the river."

There was some connection I had to establish between writing and roaming the city, between writing and my ability to react to everything in the open street. To my delight and everlasting gratitude, I was assigned by *Harper's Bazaar* to work with the photographer Henri Cartier-Bresson on a piece about the Brooklyn Bridge and the different worlds at each end of it. I was later to describe this great artist as an aristocratic radical; he was gently disdainful of the new mass housing projects crowding the view of the Lower East Side from the Brooklyn Bridge — many of them named after labor and Socialist heroes my father worshiped. But old New York, still visible in the late '40s, gave particular pleasure to Cartier-Bresson's genius eye as we walked the wooden boardwalk down the center of the bridge.

"It breathes!" Cartier-Bresson said happily about this central promenade. "See how it breathes!" With his devastating clarity and my zeal for those leftover streets we brought home the Brooklyn Bridge still anchored in the iron age, the "Swamp" district of leather factories, old assayers' shops, dealers in perfumes and wines, the ornamental fire escapes still sculptured with John L. Sullivan prize-fighter figures out of the old *Police Gazette*. Cartier-Bresson and I got on so well that we thought of doing *tout New York* in a book. But this never worked out, and I soon began writing such a book on my own.

It was very ambitious, a sort of personal epic all around New York, like *Leaves of Grass* and Hart Crane's *The Bridge*, in prose. In the first section I tried to cover morning in Pineapple Street, the blaze of midtown at noon and in the rush hour, the crowds, the museums, the libraries. The third section was all about Sunday in New York, full of color, poignance and what I thought was dazzling prose. The middle section, called "The Old Neighborhood," consisted of some dozen pages of childhood memories, which I had written in a strange burst of enthusiasm in just one afternoon but which didn't seem grand enough as a subject by comparison with midtown at noon and the city on Sunday.

What I went through for an absurdly long time trying to hammer the thing together does not deserve extended description here. But how I tried! I was a critic with a critic's weakness for ideas, and all I had then was a critic's ideas. Finally, after a ridiculously long time, I realized that I was not going to write a personal epic like *Leaves of Grass* or *The Bridge* or *Paterson* or any other of the "Columbiads" that ever since the eighteenth-century Joel Barlow have tempted our would-be Homers and Virgils. Carlyle sneered that Whitman thought he was a big poet because he lived in a big country. I suddenly opted for a small country, my natal country. The only thing emotionally authentic in my vast manuscript was those carelessly scribbled pages about growing up in Brownsville. On these, once I realized just how sensory the material really was and how vivid the prose would have to be, I could build my book.

But Brownsville — "Brunzvil," as the newly prosperous Jews long removed from it still described it? It's true that the splendid art historian Meyer Schapiro had passed through it, along with various Nobel laureates, Danny Kaye and John Garfield in East New York next door, Murder Incorporated, the crazy neighborhood thieves I actually saw skipping from roof to roof just ahead of the cops. But Brownsville? Poor ghetto Brownsville? My parents still hung on for years after the war, poor as ever. My father, no doubt praying that the spirit of Eugene Debs would forgive him, timidly complained that non-union black painters were taking work away from him at lower rates. Brownsville was now so far behind the Jews, so far behind me, that after one particularly sad Friday evening supper with my parents I wrote in my notebook, "Every time I go back it all feels like a foreign country."

But when I came to write the actual book I began: "Every

time I go back to Brownsville it is as if I had never been away." It was not behind me at all. When E. B. White removed to Maine from Manhattan he described himself as "homesick for loneliness." That was my case. As the past broke out in my book, it came to me more and more that there was no intellectual solution to my long search for the meaning of Jewishness. I would never fully fathom the hatred behind the Holocaust. I would never become pious in the orthodox Jewish fashion. I would never settle in a country that desired to be all-Jewish. I would never believe in socialism's "final conflict." I would certainly never ally myself with the financially and politically powerful or the born-again patriots who were picking up their ideologies from the ex-Left.

There was some enduring mystery, some metaphysical conundrum about being Jewish, that I was not likely to abandon. I could not get over the extraordinariness of Jewish persistence through the ages, its matter-of-fact continuity with itself, in all periods and places. The key was some heightened sense of existence, living the Jewish experience through and through. The basic fact, as my exact contemporary Saul Bellow had shown in his wonderful second book, *The Victim*, was the singularity for even a man of small gifts, in our increasingly suspicious and disenchanted world, of remaining a Jew, of remaining unsuspicious in one's deepest soul — unwearied.

Norman Mailer was to complain that the boy in *A Walker in the City* was too virtuous; Irving Howe that he did not correspond to the original facts; Lionel Trilling that the subject was a "schmo"; Oscar Handlin that there were not enough people in the book. All these Jewish sages were correct; the book astonished me, too, by going its own way. It was definitely not what anyone else would have written. But early on I realized that I was thinking in color, luxuriating in physical sensations. The breakthrough was stirring up from the depths some tangential, very slight, endlessly reverberatory memory of being taken to the old Brooklyn Children's Museum. Was it on Brooklyn Avenue? The Children's Museum had some basic connection with my first sight of Audubon's prints of birds. The museum itself, as I followed its extensive filaments in memory, was a wooden construction vaguely reminiscent of some old American farmhouse already stamped in memory as standing alone on the prairie. When I was writing my favorite section of the book, "The Block and Beyond," on my earliest walks into the city "beyond" Brownsville itself, I found myself writing:

> The day they took us to the Children's Museum — rain was dripping on the porch of that old wooden house, the halls lined with Audubon prints were hazel in the thin antique light — I was left with the distinct impression that I had been stirring between my fingers dried earth and fallen leaves that I found in between the red broken paving stones of some small American town.

From the beginning I wanted physical images, straight from the belly. In memory again — "It's memory," said Willa Cather, "the memory that goes with the vocation"

— I step off the train at Rockaway Avenue, smell the leak out of the men's room, then the pickles from the stand just below the subway steps. In these opening pages I am eager to get all the contrary feelings involved in homecoming: "an instant rage comes over me, mixed with dread and some unexpected tenderness." This is still the end of the city, the faraway place that thought of everything else as "the city," making every journey into the city a grind. Only the very old seem to have been left:

> It is always the old women in their shapeless flowered housedresses and ritual wigs I see first; they give Browns-ville back to me. In their soft dumpy bodies and the unbudging way they occupy the tenement stoops, their hands blankly folded in each other as if they had been sitting on these stoops from the beginning of time, I sense again the old foreboding that all my life would be like this.

I remember my mother's earliest complaint against me: "We are *urime yidn*, poor Jews. What do you want of us?"

But not forgetting or forgiving some early hopeless-ness, I am grabbed by the aliveness of the scene, the inex-tinguishable contrasts, the absurdity. There in the shad-ows of the El-darkened street is the torn flapping canvas sign still listing the boys who went to war, the stagnant wells of candy stores and pool parlors, the torches flaring at dusk over the vegetable stands and pushcarts, the neon-blazing fronts of liquor stores, the piles of halvah and chocolate kisses in the windows of the candy stores next to the *News* and *Mirror,* the dusty old drugstores where urns of rose and pink and blue colored water still swing from chains, and where next door Mr. A's sign still tells anyone walking down Rockaway Avenue that he has pants to fit any color suit.

These details now make me happy; the energy of the street, so much packed-up humanity, makes this tumultuously commercial street, all these automatic and violent transactions, something it is a pleasure to unravel, to make minute on paper.

> In the last crazy afternoon light the neons over the delicatessens bathe all their wares in a cosmetic smile, but strip the street of every personal shadow and concealment. The torches over the pushcarts hold in a single breath of yellow flame the acid smell of half-sour pickles and herrings floating in their briny barrels. There is a dry rattle of loose newspaper sheets around the cracked stretched skins of the "chiney" oranges. Through the kitchen windows along every ground floor I can already see the containers of milk, the fresh round poppyseed evening rolls. Time for supper, time to go home.

On this last note I have found my rhythm, the push toward home and the pull away again, the longing for the secret treasure of family and Jewish togetherness, and the contrary motion of seeking the open treasure that is the great city, infinite New York that belonged not to "us" but to "them." A key to my book is of course this constant sense of division, even of flagrant contradiction between wanting the enclosure of home *and* the open city, both moral certainty and intellectual independence. This conflict has never ended for me, I confess, which may be one reason why, thirty-six years ago in Pineapple Street, I felt that I was at last discovering an inescapable truth about myself and no doubt about other Jews of my generation brought up on the old immigrant poverty and orthodoxy. To rebel against the tradition was somehow to hold fast to it.

To want it both ways was also to span a good deal of the vehemence of Jewish history in a way perhaps unimaginable just now to those children of suburbia for whom Jewishness is psychology and troubled self-defense. Or, wearing a chic inch of *yarmulke*, relishing the ballet and the nudes at the museum of art. For me, as for so many Jewish writers and intellectual troublemakers of a certain age and condition, life in the twentieth century has been essentially political — with Jews usually at every crux of our turbulent century.

When Captain Alfred Dreyfus was accused, on the basis of forgeries gleefully committed by ultra-rightists, of betraying French military secrets to imperial Germany, he was driven out of the army in the most humiliating public ceremony. The crowd looking on hooted and shrieked, "A bas les Juifs!" The future state of Israel was in the mind of one observer in that crowd, Theodor Herzl. When Dr. Sigmund Freud in Vienna found himself virtually ostracized for his professional insights he proudly said, "Being a Jew, I knew I would be in the opposition." Leon Trotsky, Rosa Luxemburg, Gregory Zinoviev, Osip Mandelstam were confident that their being Jewish was historically insignificant; those who destroyed them did not think it insignificant. Replacing nineteenth-century illusions that the "Jewish question" would disappear under socialism, the twentieth century everywhere has seen the persecution and even the extermination of Jews wherever the state has total control. The crowd that cheered Dreyfus's disgrace was replaced by the crowd in occupied Warsaw cheering as Jews locked into the ghetto flung themselves out of windows to escape deportation.

A child of poor Russian Jews living a commonplace life in Brooklyn nevertheless feasted on every scrap of Russian memory. But beyond my innocent, literary associations with a Russian life that my parents had not really experienced themselves — imagine not speaking the language of the country you were born in! — my real passion was hearing tales of the early American West from my father. As a young immigrant painting boxcars on the Union Pacific Railroad he had gone all the way to Omaha, had heard his beloved Debs making fools of Bryan and Taft in the 1908 campaign, had been offered a homestead in Nebraska!

"Omaha" was the most beautiful word I had ever heard. "Homestead" was almost as beautiful. I could never forgive my father for not having taken that homestead.

"What would I have done there? I'm no farmer."

"You should have taken it! Why do we always live here!"

"It would have been unnatural," he wound up. "Nobody I knew."

"What a chance!"

"Don't be childish. Nobody I knew."

"Why? Why?"

"What do you want of us poor Jews?"

Under the cover of those Friday evenings, when I was about eleven, my favorite book was *The Boy's Life of Theodore Roosevelt*. Year by year T.R., the only American president born in New York City, became ever more my hero — the police commissioner who identified with a stray Jewish policeman as "straight New York," the historian and author, the only New York politician in history who could write an essay on "Dante in the Bowery." He was my guide to that other New York, the New York of Herman Melville, Henry James, Edith Wharton, Frederick Law Olmsted, Alfred Stieglitz — the New York to be achieved, in Whitman's words, by "the passage over the river." This was a New York that began at the Battery, the old Aquarium that had first been Castle Clinton, then Castle Garden, which before it became the immigrant receiving station had been the opera house where Whitman had been intoxicated by Italian sopranos.

"Beyond," as I wrote, "was anything old and American — the name *Fraunces Tavern* repeated to us on a school excursion; the eighteenth-century muskets and glazed oil paintings on the wall; the very streets, the deeper you got into Brooklyn, named after generals of the Revolutionary War — Putnam, Gates, Kosciusko, DeKalb, Lafayette, Pulaski." "Beyond" was my discovery in the Brooklyn Museum of "a circular room upstairs violently ablaze with John Singer Sargent's watercolors of the Caribbean" and a long room lined with dim farmscapes of old Brooklyn itself in the early nineteenth century. "And I knew I would come back, that I would have to come back."

The more I got into my book, the happier I became getting back into the Metropolitan Museum, into the old American Wing (not so lavishly laid out as it is now). Far in the back, in an alcove near the freight elevator, hung so low and the figures so dim in the faint light that I crouched to take them in, were pictures of New York sometime after the Civil War. Skaters in Central Park, a red muffler flying in the wind; a gay crowd moving round and round Union Square Park; horsecars charging between the brownstones of lower Fifth Avenue at dusk. I couldn't believe my eyes. Room on room they had painted my city, and this city was my country: Winslow Homer's dark oblong of Union soldiers making camp in the rain, tenting tonight, tenting on the old campground, as I had never thought I would get to see them when we sang that song in school; Thomas Eakins's solitary sculler on the Schuylkill, resting to have his portrait painted in the yellow light bright with patches of raw spring in Pennsylvania showing on the other side of him. Most wonderful to me then was John Sloan's picture of a young girl standing in the wind on the deck of a New York ferryboat — surely to Staten Island, and just about the year of my birth? — looking out to water.

America between the Civil War and the "Great War" was to become my favorite period for study. When I eventually discovered Lewis Mumford's *The Brown Decades*, a prime book on the subject, with its loving portraits of Emily Dickinson, John Augustus Roebling, the creator of the Brooklyn Bridge, and the painter Albert Pinkham Ryder (in those days you could still see on University Place the Hotel Albert, named after the mystical painter by his brother), I was hooked for life. It had everything to do with such historical items as Park Row on a winter afternoon in the 1880s, the snow falling into the dark stone streets under the Brooklyn Bridge, newsboys running under the maze of telegraph wires that darkened every street of the lower city. How those wires haunted me in every photograph I found of old New York. Indescribably heavy, they sagged between the poles; the very streets seemed to sink under their weight. The past was that forest of wires hung over lower New York at five o'clock.

Ever more vivid to me as the years went on were certain prime figures moving against that dark, brooding landscape: Melville the customs inspector checking cargoes on newly arrived ships all along the Hudson up to Harlem, bitter at the ignoramuses who didn't know that Gansevoort Street, where Melville took his lunch, was named after his own grandfather, the Revolutionary War hero. Later, seeing the ghosts of New York writers in *their* old neighborhoods, it was easy to imagine Mark Twain still living at Tenth Street and Fifth Avenue, more picturesque than anyone else as, with silk hat perched on his snowy white hair (washed every morning with laundry soap), he walked up Fifth Avenue just ahead of the crowd that always recognized and followed him. And finally, joining one past to another, there was Henry James on his native's return to the Lower East Side of New York in 1905, studying the fire escapes heaped with Jewish immigrants just like my father and mother. He would describe them all in that most majestic of travel books, *The American Scene*. But unlike me he would see them only in the mass, as faintly repellent intruders, agents of "future ravage."

All this did not complete the circle of memories; my forays into the past continued with *Starting Out in the Thirties* and *New York Jew*. Now, past seventy, I am still trying to make a book out of my lifetime notebooks called *Too Much Happens*. Mrs. Hines, Joe Christmas's grandmother in Faulkner's *Light in August*, muses after his death: "It is because so much happens. Too much happens." What happens every day, virtually every moment, can be an amazement still that I have to put down in writing. Let the future decipher it. My involvement with so much personal history has this excuse: It is about someone taken up in history, someone who was in history — like all his people — before he was born. And I cannot fully explain the necessity, which can be more unnerving to me than to the people I write about. But recently there was a moment when I felt repaid for all my struggles.

A Walker in the City is much used in composition courses, and while I was still teaching at Hunter College I was asked by some freshman students to answer questions about the book. A black girl said to me, a little angrily: "I come from Amboy and Sutter. I sure know the place. Teach me to write like that."

TONI MORRISON

The Site of Memory

My inclusion in a series of talks on autobiography and memoir is not entirely a misalliance. Although it's probably true that a fiction writer thinks of his or her work as alien in that company, what I have to say may suggest why I'm not completely out of place here. For one thing, I might throw into relief the differences between self-recollection (memoir) and fiction, and also some of the similarities — the places where those two crafts embrace and where that embrace is symbiotic.

But the authenticity of my presence here lies in the fact that a very large part of my own literary heritage is the autobiography. In this country the print origins of black literature (as distinguished from the oral origins) were slave narratives. These book-length narratives (autobiographies, recollections, memoirs), of which well over a hundred were published, are familiar texts to historians and students of black history. They range from the adventure-packed life of Olaudah Equiano's *The Interesting Narrative of the Life of Olaudah Equiano, or Gustavus Vassa, the African, Written by Himself* (1769) to the quiet desperation of *Incidents in the Life of a Slave Girl: Written by Herself* (1861), in which Harriet Jacob ("Linda Brent") records hiding for seven years in a room too small to stand up in; from the political savvy of Frederick Douglass's *Narrative of the Life of Frederick Douglass, an American Slave, Written by Himself* (1845) to the subtlety and modesty of Henry Bibb, whose voice, in *Life and Adventures of Henry Bibb, an American Slave, Written by Himself* (1849), is surrounded by ("loaded with" is a better phrase) documents attesting to its authenticity. Bibb is careful to note that his formal schooling (three weeks) was short, but that he was "educated in the school of adversity, whips, and chains." Born in Kentucky, he put aside his plans to escape in order to marry. But when he learned that he was the father of a slave and watched the degradation of his wife and child, he reactivated those plans.

Whatever the style and circumstances of these narratives, they were written to say principally two things. One: "This is my historical life — my singular, special example that is personal, but that also represents the race." Two: "I write this text to persuade other people — you, the reader, who is probably not black — that we are human beings worthy of God's grace and the immediate abandonment of slavery." With these two missions in mind, the narratives were clearly pointed.

In Equiano's account, the purpose is quite up-front. Born in 1745 near the Niger River and captured at the age of ten, he survived the Middle Passage, American plantation slavery, wars in Canada and the Mediterranean; learned navigation and clerking from a Quaker named Robert King, and bought his freedom at twenty-one. He lived as a free servant, traveling widely and living most of his latter life in England. Here he is speaking to the British without equivocation: "I hope to have the satisfaction of seeing the renovation of liberty and justice resting on the British government. . . . I hope and expect the attention of gentlemen of power. . . . May the time come — at least the speculation is to me pleasing — when the sable people shall gratefully commemorate the auspicious era of extensive freedom." With typically eighteenth-century reticence he records his singular and representative life for one purpose: to change things. In fact, he and his coauthors *did* change things. Their works gave fuel to the fires that abolitionists were setting everywhere.

More difficult was getting the fair appraisal of literary critics. The writings of church martyrs and confessors are and were read for the eloquence of their message as well as their experience of redemption, but the American slaves' autobiographical narratives were frequently scorned as "biased," "inflammatory" and "improbable." These attacks are particularly difficult to understand in view of the fact that it was extremely important, as you can imagine, for the writers of these narratives to appear as objective as possible — not to offend the reader by being too angry, or by showing too much outrage, or by calling the reader names. As recently as 1966, Paul Edwards, who edited and abridged Equiano's story, praises the narrative for its refusal to be "inflammatory."

"As a rule," Edwards writes, "he [Equiano] puts no emotional pressure on the reader other than that which the situation itself contains — his language does not strain after our sympathy, but expects it to be given naturally and at the proper time. This quiet avoidance of emotional display produces many of the best passages in the book." Similarly, an 1836 review of Charles Bell's *Life and Adventures of a Fugitive Slave*, which appeared in the "Quarterly Anti-Slavery Magazine," praised Bell's account for its objectivity. "We rejoice in the book the more, because it is not a partisan work. . . . It broaches no theory in regard to [slavery], nor proposes any mode or time of emancipation."

As determined as these black writers were to persuade the reader of the evil of slavery, they also complimented him by assuming his nobility of heart and his high-mindedness. They tried to summon up his finer nature in order to encourage him to employ it. They knew that their readers were the people who could make a difference in terminating slavery. Their stories — of brutality, adversity and deliverance — had great popularity in spite of critical hostility in many quarters and patronizing sympathy in others. There was a time when the hunger for "slave stories" was difficult to quiet, as sales figures show. Douglass's *Narrative* sold five thousand copies in four months; by 1847 it had sold eleven thousand copies. Equiano's book had thirty-six editions between 1789 and 1850. Moses Roper's book had ten editions from 1837 to 1856; William Wells Brown's was reprinted four times in its first year. Solomon Northrop's book sold twenty-seven thousand copies before two years had passed. A book by Josiah Henson (argued by some to be the model for the "Tom" of Harriet Beecher Stowe's *Uncle Tom's Cabin*) had a pre-publication sale of five thousand.

In addition to using their own lives to expose the horrors of slavery, they had a companion motive for their efforts. The prohibition against teaching a slave to read and write (which in many Southern states carried severe punishment) and against a slave's learning to read and write had to be scuttled at all costs. These writers knew that literacy was power. Voting, after all, was inextricably connected to the ability to read; literacy was a way of assuming and proving the "humanity" that the Constitution denied them. That is why the narratives carry the subtitle "written by himself," or "herself," and include introductions and prefaces by white sympathizers to authenticate them. Other narratives, "edited by" such well-known anti-slavery figures as Lydia Maria Child and John Greenleaf Whittier, contain prefaces to assure the reader how little editing was needed. A literate slave was supposed to be a contradiction in terms.

One has to remember that the climate in which they wrote reflected not only the Age of Enlightenment but its twin, born at the same time, the Age of Scientific Racism. David Hume, Immanuel Kant and Thomas Jefferson, to mention only a few, had documented their conclusions that blacks were incapable of intelligence. Frederick Douglass knew otherwise, and he wrote refutations of what Jefferson said in "Notes on the State of Virginia": "Never yet could I find that a black had uttered a thought above the level of plain narration, never see even an elementary trait of painting or sculpture" — a sentence that I have always thought ought to be engraved at the door to the Rockefeller Collection of African Art. Hegel, in 1813, had said that Africans had no "history" and couldn't write in modern languages. Kant disregarded a perceptive observation by a black man by saying, "This fellow was quite black from head to foot, a clear proof that what he said was stupid."

Yet no slave society in the history of the world wrote more — or more thoughtfully — about its own enslavement. The milieu, however, dictated the purpose and the style. The narratives are instructive, moral and obviously representative. Some of them are patterned after the sentimental novel that was in vogue at the time. But whatever the level of eloquence or the form, popular taste discouraged the writers from dwelling too long or too carefully on the more sordid details of their experience. Whenever there was an unusually violent incident, or a scatological one, or something "excessive," one finds the writer taking refuge in the literary conventions of the day. "I was left in a state of distraction not to be described" (Equiano). "But let us now leave the rough usage of the field . . . and turn our attention to the less repulsive slave life as it existed in the house of my childhood" (Douglass). "I am not about to harrow the feelings of my readers by a terrific representation of the untold horrors of that fearful system of oppression. . . . It is not my purpose to descend deeply into the dark and noisome caverns of the hell of slavery" (Henry Box Brown).

Over and over, the writers pull the narrative up short with a phrase such as, "But let us drop a veil over these proceedings too terrible to relate." In shaping the experience to make it palatable to those who were in a position to alleviate it, they were silent about many things, and they "forgot" many other things. There was a careful selection of the instances that they would record and a careful rendering of those that they chose to describe. Lydia Maria Child identified the problem in her introduction to "Linda Brent's" tale of sexual abuse: "I am well aware that many will accuse me of indecorum for presenting these pages to the public; for the experiences of this intelligent and much-injured woman belong to a class which some call delicate subjects, and others indelicate. This peculiar phase of Slavery has generally been kept veiled; but the public ought to be made acquainted with its monstrous features, and I am willing to take the responsibility of presenting them with the veil drawn [aside]."

But most importantly — at least for me — there was no mention of their interior life.

For me — a writer in the last quarter of the twentieth century, not much more than a hundred years after Emancipation, a writer who is black and a woman — the exercise is very different. My job becomes how to rip that veil drawn over "proceedings too terrible to relate." The exercise is also critical for any person who is black, or who belongs to any marginalized category, for, historically, we were seldom invited to participate in the discourse even when we were its topic.

Moving that veil aside requires, therefore, certain things. First of all, I must trust my own recollections. I must also depend on the recollections of others. Thus memory weighs heavily in what I write, in how I begin and in what I find to be significant. Zora Neale Hurston said, "Like the dead-seeming cold rocks, I have memories within that came out of the material that went to make me." These "memories within" are the subsoil of my work. But memories and recollections won't give me total access to the unwritten interior life of these people. Only the act of the imagination can help me.

If writing is thinking and discovery and selection and order and meaning, it is also awe and reverence and mystery and magic. I suppose I could dispense with the last four if I were not so deadly serious about fidelity to the milieu out of which I write and in which my ancestors actually lived. Infidelity to that milieu — the absence of the interior life, the deliberate excising of it from the records that the slaves themselves told — is precisely the problem in the discourse that proceeded without us. How I gain access to that interior life is what drives me and is the part of this talk which both distinguishes my fiction from autobiographical strategies and which also embraces certain autobiographical strategies. It's a kind of literary archeology: On the basis of some information and a little bit of guesswork you journey to a site to see what remains were left behind and to reconstruct the world that these remains imply. What makes it fiction is the nature of the imaginative act: my reliance on the image — on the remains — in addition to recollection, to yield up a kind of a truth. By "image," of course, I don't mean "symbol"; I simply mean "picture" and the feelings that accompany the picture.

Fiction, by definition, is distinct from fact. Presumably it's the product of imagination — invention — and it claims the freedom to dispense with "what really happened," or where it really happened, or when it really happened, and nothing in it needs to be publicly verifiable, although much in it can be verified. By contrast, the scholarship of the biographer and the literary critic seems to us only trustworthy when the events of fiction can be traced to some publicly verifiable fact. It's the research of the "Oh, yes, this is where he or she got it from" school, which gets its own credibility from excavating the credibility of the sources of the imagination, not the nature of the imagination.

The work that I do frequently falls, in the minds of most people, into that realm of fiction called fantastic, or mythic, or magical, or unbelievable. I'm not comfortable with these labels. I consider that my single gravest responsibility (in spite of that magic) is not to lie. When I hear someone say, "Truth is stranger than fiction," I think that old chestnut is truer than we know, because it doesn't say that truth is truer than fiction; just that it's stranger, meaning that it's odd. It may be excessive, it may be more interesting, but the important thing is that it's random — and fiction is not random.

Therefore the crucial distinction for me is not the difference between fact and fiction, but the distinction between fact and truth. Because facts can exist without human intelligence, but truth cannot. So if I'm looking to find and expose a truth about the interior life of people who didn't write it (which doesn't mean that they didn't have it); if I'm trying to fill in the blanks that the slave narratives left — to part the veil that was so frequently drawn, to implement the stories that I heard — then the approach that's most productive and most trustworthy for me is the recollection that moves from the image to the text. Not from the text to the image.

Simone de Beauvoir, in *A Very Easy Death*, says, "I don't know why I was so shocked by my mother's death." When she heard her mother's name being called at the funeral by the priest, she says, "Emotion seized me by the throat. . . . 'Françoise de Beauvoir': the words brought her to life; they summed up her history, from birth to marriage to widowhood to the grave. Françoise de Beauvoir — that retiring woman, so rarely named, became an *important* person." The book becomes an exploration both into her own grief and into the images in which the grief lay buried.

Unlike Mme. de Beauvoir, Frederick Douglass asks the reader's patience for spending about half a page on the death of his grandmother — easily the most profound loss he had suffered — and he apologizes by saying, in effect, "It really was very important to me. I hope you aren't bored by my indulgence." He makes no attempt to explore that death: its images or its meaning. His narrative is as close to factual as he can make it, which leaves no room for subjective speculation. James Baldwin, on the other hand, in *Notes of a Native Son*, says, in recording his father's life and his own relationship to his father, "All of my father's Biblical texts and songs, which I had decided were meaningless, were ranged before me at his death like empty bottles, waiting to hold the meaning which life would give them for me." And then his text fills those bottles. Like Simone de Beauvoir, he moves from the event to the image that it left. My route is the reverse: The image comes first and tells me what the "memory" is about.

I can't tell you how I felt when my father died. But I was able to write *Song of Solomon* and imagine, not him, and not his specific interior life, but the world that he inhabited and the private or interior life of the people in it. And I can't tell you how I felt reading to my grandmother while she was turning over and over in her bed (because she was dying, and she was not comfortable), but I could try to reconstruct the world that she lived in. And I have suspected, more often than not, that *I know* more than she did, that *I know* more than my grandfather and my great-grandmother did, but I also know that I'm no wiser than they were. And whenever I have tried earnestly to diminish their vision and prove to myself that I know more, and when I have tried to speculate on their interior life and match it up with my own, I have been overwhelmed every time by the richness of theirs compared to my own. Like Frederick Douglass talking about his grandmother, and James Baldwin talking about his father, and Simone de Beauvoir talking about her mother, these people are my access to me; they are my entrance into my own interior life. Which is why the images that float around them — the remains, so to speak, at the archeological site — surface first, and they surface so vividly and so compellingly that I acknowledge them as my route to a reconstruction of a world, to an exploration of an interior life that was not written and to the revelation of a kind of truth.

So the nature of my research begins with something as

ineffable and as flexible as a dimly recalled figure, the corner of a room, a voice. I began to write my second book, which was called *Sula*, because of my preoccupation with a picture of a woman and the way in which I heard her name pronounced. Her name was Hannah, and I think she was a friend of my mother's. I don't remember seeing her very much, but what I do remember is the color around her — a kind of violet, a suffusion of something violet — and her eyes, which appeared to be half closed. But what I remember most is how the women said her name: how they said "Hannah Peace" and smiled to themselves, and there was some secret about her that they knew, which they didn't talk about, at least not in my hearing, but it seemed *loaded* in the way in which they said her name. And I suspected that she was a little bit of an outlaw but that they approved in some way.

And then, thinking about their relationship to her and the way in which they talked about her, the way in which they articulated her name, made me think about friendship between women. What is it that they forgive each other for? And what it is that is unforgivable in the world of women. I don't want to know any more about Miss Hannah Peace, and I'm not going to ask my mother who she really was and what did she do and what were you laughing about and why were you smiling? Because my experience when I do this with my mother is so crushing: She will give you *the* most pedestrian information you ever heard, and I would like to keep all of my remains and my images intact in their mystery when I begin. Later I will get to the facts. That way I can explore two worlds — the actual and the possible.

What I want to do in this talk is to track an image from picture to meaning to text — a journey which appears in the novel that I'm writing now, which is called *Beloved*.

I'm trying to write a particular kind of scene, and I see corn on the cob. To "see" corn on the cob doesn't mean that it suddenly hovers; it only means that it keeps coming back. And in trying to figure out "What is all this corn doing?" I discover what it *is* doing.

I see the house where I grew up in Lorain, Ohio. My parents had a garden some distance away from our house, and they didn't welcome me and my sister there, when we were young, because we were not able to distinguish between the things that they wanted to grow and the things that they didn't, so we were not able to hoe, or weed, until much later.

I see them walking, together, away from me. I'm looking at their backs and what they're carrying in their arms: their tools, and maybe a peck basket. Sometimes when they walk away from me they hold hands, and they go to this other place in the garden. They have to cross some railroad tracks to get there.

I also am aware that my mother and father sleep at odd hours because my father works many jobs and works at night. And these naps are times of pleasure for me and my sister because nobody's giving us chores, or telling us what to do, or nagging us in any way. In addition to which, there is some feeling of pleasure in them that I'm only vaguely aware of. They're very rested when they take these naps.

And later on in the summer we have an opportunity to eat corn, which is the one plant that I can distinguish from the others, and which is the harvest that I like the best; the others are the food that no child likes — the collards, the okra, the strong, violent vegetables that I would give a great deal for now. But I do like the corn because it's sweet, and because we all sit down to eat it, and it's finger food, and it's hot, and it's even good cold, and there are neighbors in, and there are uncles in, and it's easy, and it's nice.

The picture of the corn and the nimbus of emotion surrounding it became a powerful one in the manuscript I'm now completing.

Authors arrive at text and subtext in thousands of ways, learning each time they begin anew how to recognize a valuable idea and how to render the texture that accompanies, reveals or displays it to its best advantage. The process by which this is accomplished is endlessly fascinating to me. I have always thought that as an editor for twenty years I understood writers better than their most careful critics, because in examining the manuscript in each of its subsequent stages I knew the author's process, how his or her mind worked, what was effortless, what took time, where the "solution" to a problem came from. The end result — the book — was all that the critic had to go on.

Still, for me, that was the least important aspect of the work. Because, no matter how "fictional" the account of these writers, or how much it was a product of invention, the act of imagination is bound up with memory. You know, they straightened out the Mississippi River in places, to make room for houses and livable acreage. Occasionally the river floods these places. "Floods" is the word they use, but in fact it is not flooding; it is remembering. Remembering where it used to be. All water has a perfect memory and is forever trying to get back to where it was. Writers are like that: remembering where we were, what valley we ran through, what the banks were like, the light that was there and the route back to our original place. It is emotional memory — what the nerves and the skin remember as well as how it appeared. And a rush of imagination is our "flooding."

Along with personal recollection, the matrix of the work I do is the wish to extend, fill in and complement slave autobiographical narratives. But only the matrix. What comes of all that is dictated by other concerns, not least among them the novel's own integrity. Still, like water, I remember where I was before I was "straightened out."

*

Q. I would like to ask about your point of view as a novelist. Is it a vision, or are you taking the part of the particular characters?

I try sometimes to have genuinely minor characters just walk through, like a walk-on actor. But I get easily distracted by them, because a novelist's imagination goes like that: Every little road looks to me like an adventure, and once you begin to claim it and describe it, it looks like more, and you invent more and more and more. I don't mind doing that in my first draft, but afterward I have to cut back. I have seen myself get distracted, and people have loomed much larger than I had planned, and minor characters have seemed a little bit more interesting than they need to be for the purposes of the book. In that case I try to endow them: If there are little pieces of information that I want to reveal, I let them do some of the work. But I try not to get carried away; I try to restrain it, so that, finally, the texture is consistent and nothing is wasted; there are no words in the final text that are unnecessary, and no people who are not absolutely necessary.

As for the point of view, there should be the illusion that it's the characters' point of view, when in fact it isn't; it's really the narrator who is there but who doesn't make herself (in my case) known in that role. I like the feeling of a *told* story, where you hear a voice but you can't identify it, and you think it's your own voice. It's a comfortable voice, and it's a guiding voice, and it's alarmed by the same things that the reader is alarmed by, and it doesn't know what's going to happen next either. So you have this sort of guide. But that guide can't have a personality; it can only have a sound, and you have to feel comfortable with this voice, and then this voice can easily abandon itself and reveal the interior dialogue of a character. So it's a combination of using the point of view of various characters but still retaining the power to slide in and out, provided that when I'm "out" the reader doesn't see little fingers pointing to what's in the text.

What I really want is that intimacy in which the reader is under the impression that he isn't really reading this; that he is participating in it as he goes along. It's unfolding, and he's always two beats ahead of the characters and right on target.

Q. You have said that writing is a solitary activity. Do you go into steady seclusion when you're writing, so that your feelings are sort of contained, or do you have to get away, and go out shopping and . . . ?

I do all of it. I've been at this book for three years. I go out shopping, and I stare, and I do whatever. It goes away. Sometimes it's very intense and I walk — I mean, I write a sentence and I jump up and run outside or something; it sort of beats you up. And sometimes I don't. Sometimes I write long hours every day. I get up at 5:30 and just go do it, and if I don't like it the next day, I throw it away. But I sit down and do it. By now I know how to get to that place where something is working. I didn't always know; I thought every thought I had was interesting — because it was mine. Now I know better how to throw away things that are not useful. I can stand around and do other things and think about it at the same time. I don't mind not writing every minute; I'm not so terrified.

When you first start writing — and I think it's true for a lot of beginning writers — you're scared to death that if you don't get that sentence right that minute it's never going to show up again. And it isn't. But it doesn't matter — another one will, and it'll probably be better. And I don't mind writing badly for a couple of days because I know I can fix it — and fix it again and again and again, and it will be better. I don't have the hysteria that used to accompany some of those dazzling passages that I thought the world was just dying for me to remember. I'm a little more sanguine about it now. Because the best part of it all, the absolutely most delicious part, is finishing it and then doing it over. That's the thrill of a lifetime for me: if I can just get done with that first phase and then have infinite time to fix it and change it. I rewrite a lot, over and over again, so that it looks like I never did. I try to make it look like I never touched it, and that takes a lot of time and a lot of sweat.

Q. In *Song of Solomon,* what was the relationship between your memories and what you made up? Was it very tenuous?

Yes, it was tenuous. For the first time I was writing a book in which the central stage was occupied by men, and which had something to do with my loss, or my perception of loss, of a man (my father) and the world that disappeared with him. (It didn't, but *I felt* that it did.) So I was re-creating a time period that was his — not biographically his life or anything in it; I use whatever's around. But it seemed to me that there was this big void after he died, and I filled it with a book that was about men because my two previous books had had women as the central characters. So in that sense it was about my memories and the need to invent. I had to do something. I was in such a rage because my father was dead. The connections between us were threads that I either mined for a lot of strength or they were purely invention. But I created a male world and inhabited it and it had this quest — a journey from stupidity to epiphany, of a man, a complete man. It was my way of exploring all that, of trying to figure out what he may have known.

EILEEN SIMPSON

Poets in My Youth

As the Russian poet Anna Akhmatova said, every attempt to produce a coherent memoir amounts to falsification. No human memory is so arranged as to recollect everything in continuous sequence, and letters and diaries often turn out to be untrustworthy assistants. Because *Poets in Their Youth* was not a memoir of my own life but of a group of poets I had known when I was a young woman married to the poet John Berryman, I had to rely on a good deal of external material, some of it trustworthy, some of it needing verification.

The book had its genesis when I was a graduate student in psychology. I had been struggling to find an interesting project for a thesis. One day, in the middle of a class on the Rorschach inkblot test, our professor was bemoaning the fact that there were no studies of creative people, especially poets, because they're so hard to approach and so reluctant to be tested. (In a Rorschach test the subject's responses to the blots provide a kind of x-ray of his psychic strengths and weaknesses.) I thought, "Here's the perfect subject for my thesis, just tossed into my lap. I'll interview the poets I've met through John."

It was a bit tricky, because I wasn't sure they would cooperate — they were tremendously suspicious of psychotherapy and psychoanalysis, though some of them went through it themselves at one time or another. To my surprise and delight, all of them — Allen Tate, R. P. Blackmur, Robert Lowell, Randall Jarrell, Delmore Schwartz, W. S. Merwin, William Carlos Williams, and of course John Berryman — agreed to talk to me.

Williams was the only one I didn't know, but I was particularly eager to include him in my study because he was also a practicing pediatrician. I wrote to him rather uneasily. He wrote back saying that he'd be glad to see me the following Sunday. John could come along, he said, and we would have lunch and make a day of it. All the way to Rutherford, New Jersey, I kept saying to John, "How am I going to get him to talk about his life?" John, who was somewhat worried himself about meeting Williams, said, "I know *I* wouldn't talk if a stranger and a psychologist came to see *me*." Not very reassuring.

Well, we got off the train and Dr. Williams met us in a beat-up Plymouth that he used for making house calls, with his black medical bag in the front seat, and he began to talk autobiographically and he never stopped. He told me about his recent heart attack, about his children, and about his patients. He continued to talk all through lunch;

his wife and his adult son hardly got a word in. After lunch I had to remind him that he and I had business. We went upstairs to his study, where I gave him the Rorschach, which took two hours, and came back down, and he continued talking as he drove us to the train — all the way to the station. When we got there he said, "You're going *too soon* — there's so much I haven't told you." At that time John was working on a biography of Stephen Crane. When we got on the train he said, "You know more about Williams after one afternoon than I do about Crane after two years of research."

After I finished my thesis — this was in 1950 — I thought I might develop the material into a more extended psychological study. I started a file called "Poets." I put newspaper clippings about them into the file, along with my own notes on their conversations, their triumphs and their troubles. But my psychotherapy practice became so demanding that I didn't have time for anything else, and then, in the 1960s, I went abroad to live. It wasn't until 1980, after I finished writing *Reversals*, my memoir about dyslexia, that I looked through the "Poets" file and realized that over the years I had collected a wealth of material that would be useful for a book.

I couldn't use the Rorschachs, because they were confidential, but a great deal of information about these writers was now in the public domain, or soon would be. Biographies of the poets were beginning to appear. I also had their own writing — not only their poetry but their fiction, literary criticism and various autobiographical fragments such as Lowell's *Life Studies*. I reread everything they had published. That's when I decided to write a memoir rather than a psychological study.

Just then I had an interesting experience. I had applied for a month's stay at Yaddo, the artists' colony in Saratoga Springs, where I hoped to write a first draft of one or two early chapters. But as I drove up there I decided that I wouldn't start at the beginning. Instead I would try to write what I felt would be a crucial chapter, recalling a summer visit that John Berryman and I made to Jean Stafford and Robert Lowell, who were then married. They had bought a house in Damariscotta Mills, Maine, and were so delighted to own something that they invited various guests. Jean wrote a fictional version of that summer in a short story called "An Influx of Poets."

My sister Marie had recently told me, when I mentioned that I was planning to write a memoir, that she had kept all the letters I had written her during the years when I was married to John. That astonished me, because I throw everything out. But now, when I told her I was going to Yaddo and needed the letters, she looked everywhere and couldn't find them. (She had moved three times.)

At Yaddo I learned right away that if you're going to write a memoir about other people you need all the documentation you can get — to check your memories and enrich them. Every night as I went over what I had written I found myself thinking, "This is too thin!" What *exactly* did we have for dinner? What did the poets talk about as we sat up till 2 A.M.? Those details would have interested my sister; I would have written about such things to her. I *needed* those letters. Without them my confidence began to drain away and I thought perhaps I should abandon the whole project. This agonizing had gone on for about a week when I got a call from my sister. She had found my letters in a cardboard carton in the attic. Her husband had used it as a prop for the attic fan.

I also learned something else at Yaddo that was tremendously important for the writer of a memoir, or at least for me. I found that the best way to stimulate a memory of the past was to assume the position of a person being psychoanalyzed — to lie on a couch and associate freely, just as a patient does during an analytical hour. Luckily, every studio at Yaddo comes furnished with a couch as well as a desk and a chair. So I would lie on the couch and try to think my way back to 1947. I would wait to see what came up on the memory screen, as people do when they're recalling dreams or other experiences. It was like waiting under water for a certain species of fish to swim by.

If anyone had dropped in to my studio they would have thought I was taking a nap or goofing off. But in fact the effort of trying to recall the past was hard work — every bit as hard as writing. Sometimes an hour would pass and nothing would come, so I'd get up and do something else: have lunch or go for a walk. Then I'd try again. Finally, one day, I remembered with great clarity a Sunday when the Lowells and I went to church together. I saw the inverted funnel of the hat Jean was wearing. I saw "Cal" Lowell's untied shoelaces. I saw Cal taking me to the cemetery after mass — the cemetery that would later appear in his poem, "The Mills of the Kavanaghs."

So I had at least done some preparatory work before I went back to New York, where my letters to Marie were waiting for me. It was a blistering hot August in New York, and I was holed up in my apartment with that cardboard carton. At first I didn't want to open it; the past was in that box — much of it painful — ready to spring out at me. Even the smell of the letters made me queasy; everything was moldy. The period that was covered in those letters had ended in my separation from John Berryman. It was also the beginning of an increasingly turbulent period for some of the poets, leading to alcoholism and breakdowns and tragic deaths. In my book I wanted to return to a time when they were young and full of hope and ambition and promise. That's why I took my title from Wordsworth's lines:

We poets in our youth begin in gladness
But thereof comes in the end despondency and
    madness.

I remembered that my thesis professor had looked at those Rorschachs and said, "I can hardly believe that these men have been so productive, because there's so much pathology," and I said, "But that's the point." Despite the psychological burdens, those poets had so much psychic energy that they were able to overcome adversity. Unlike many people who go through a severe depression, they were able to come back. Robert Lowell would come out of the hospital after a terrible episode, and in a year or two he'd be writing again. That was the striking thing I learned from the Rorschachs of those poets. They had psychic energy in abundance.

I stalled by counting my letters to Marie — there were more than six hundred. They were messy and full of typos and misspellings. I had only meant them as an attempt to entertain my sister, who was then housebound with three children and having a difficult time. We couldn't afford telephone calls — it wasn't cheap in those days — and being married to a poet, I sometimes didn't even have a telephone. I was a graduate student with a part-time job at a clinic at Rutgers, and I would just knock these letters out on my lunch hour while eating my peanut butter sandwich.

My letters turned out to be rich in exactly the kind of detail I needed: what Jean Stafford gave us for dinner, how the poets looked and dressed, their mannerisms, their wit, their moods. The letters were also undated. That was something I didn't forgive myself for — chronology is very important in this kind of writing, and I couldn't trust my memory. Fortunately, my orderly sister had saved the letters in their envelopes, so I had the postmarks. Those postmarks were a very helpful assistant.

After *Poets in Their Youth* was published, people asked me how I could remember so many anecdotes, some of them quite lengthy. I think it was because the poets made a group and they were gossips. No matter where they lived, they kept in touch with one another, by mail and through the grapevine, in a friendly and competitive way, and they passed the news along. Robert Lowell once said that there's nothing so refreshing after a hard day of work as gossip. They loved it. When one of them began an affair or won a prize or had a breakdown, the news traveled fast among the others. If you listened, as I did, you heard the stories more than once, and repetition deepens the memory grooves.

I didn't listen to those poets because I thought that one day I'd write about them. That never occurred to me. I listened because they fascinated me. I had never met anyone like them. Why did they behave the way they did? That got me interested in motivation and showed me what I wanted to study in graduate school and what I wanted to do with my life — to become a psychotherapist. It also made me a very attentive listener. I was the shy one in that group; although the poets weren't much older than I was, they seemed much older — they were so articulate. They also had big egos and were big talkers; they weren't unhappy to have someone listening to everything they said.

Many readers have commented that my book is very forgiving and nonjudgmental. They say, "Those poets were so irresponsible and destructive of people's lives; how could you resist saying, 'Would you believe how terribly they behaved?'" You have to understand that I was so admiring of them. I was just out of college when I went to be a faculty wife at Harvard. I felt about those writers the way other young women of that age felt about movie stars. I was dazzled by their learning, their wit and their charm. Oh, those people were so seductive! Remember, too, that I was writing about them in the "gladness" of their youth. The problems came later — the breakdowns and the chaos in their lives. If I had met them for the first time when they were older I'm sure I wouldn't have found them so attractive.

Also, as a psychotherapist you can't be judgmental. In this book I was like an anthropologist who studies a tribe and reports what she finds, trying to be as objective as possible. Those poets *were* like a tribe; they were as exotic to me as the people Margaret Mead wrote about. I had never met people of such complexity. They weren't like other people and they *were* like each other. They had what Lowell called their "generic" life.

My problem was how to tell the truth about them without patronizing them, or focusing on pathology. I was writing a memoir, not a psychological study. I didn't want to write as a therapist, or to write what Joyce Carol Oates calls "pathography." My aim was to recapture the excitement of those extremely gifted young men. I wanted to make them as attractive to the reader as they had been to me. On the other hand, I wanted to be accurate.

The first draft was a near disaster. My editor sent it back and said, "*You* aren't in the book enough." What I had left out was my take on it. He said, "You were there, you were involved. You have to tell us what you thought and what you felt." I put the manuscript aside and didn't look at it for three months. Then I read it straight through and thought, "I don't know why my editor even bothered to talk to me about this version — it's so wooden." I was in a funk for about three days. Then I decided, "I'm going to rewrite it," and I rewrote the whole book from beginning to end, with hardly a glance back at what I had done before.

This time I wrote in a much more confident tone. In my first draft the writing had been timorous: I was the twenty-three-year-old girl sitting at the feet of these great men. When my editor told me to put myself in the book I began to write as the older woman I now was, not as the tentative young faculty wife. It's an easy trap for a memoir writer to fall into. You're trying to reconstruct something that happened when you were much more unformed, but as an artist you have to be true to the older and wiser person you have become.

When the book was reviewed, most older critics and poets wrote favorably about it. The next younger group — people in their forties — were less enthusiastic. They thought I was being hypercritical. One English reviewer took me to task for calling John Berryman "obsessive." But of course John *was* obsessive; when he was working on something he was so thoroughly concentrated on it that he thought of nothing else. Sometimes he had to be reminded to eat and sleep. The poets I wrote about had a tremendous effect on the generation that followed them. Many of those younger poets decided that they weren't going to risk living the "madness" of my poets' later years just for the sake of writing poetry. Their poems are more cautious. Two of them told me they gave up writing poetry altogether because they wanted to have a normal life.

*

Q. Let's talk about your other two memoirs, *Reversals* and *Orphans*, which preceded and followed *Poets in Their Youth* and are much more personal because they deal with your own childhood and its two central traumas — being severely dyslexic and being an orphan.

When I began writing *Poets*, I thought it was going to be hard for me to read my old letters and confront the past. But I soon found that I could deal with that. *Reversals* and *Orphans*, on the other hand, turned out to be much more difficult and painful.

To write *Reversals* I had to reveal a humiliating secret: that as a child I couldn't learn to read. My adult life has been lived in academic and literary circles, where I'm surrounded by people who were the top students from kindergarten through graduate school; they learned to read before they even started school and won all the gold stars once they got there. I had always taken care to conceal from them the stigma of my early years, my resulting retardation as a student and my continuing struggle to cope with this disability. I hid it even from my close friends. I was afraid I would be patronized.

When I wrote *Reversals*, about fifteen years ago, there was little popular understanding of what dyslexia is. Nothing had been written from the dyslexic's point of view — nothing that a dyslexic child or his parents could read. If I was going to write a memoir I knew it couldn't be from the lofty perch of a psychologist. I would have to admit that it was *my* disability and describe it in personal terms, free of professional jargon, so that people would understand what it was like to grow up this way. I resisted my editor's suggestion that I begin with a technical chapter on the neurology and psychology of the dyslexic syndrome; I would get to that information later. I wanted to write a book that I would have been willing to read as a young woman trying to figure out what was wrong with me.

One bit of research turned out to be very useful. Although I remembered vividly what it was like as a third grader not to be able to make sense out of a page of print — even a phrase as simple as "Jack and Jill went up the hill" — it was hard for me to imagine what it was like for teachers who had me as a pupil. So I asked if I could visit a clinic in Princeton that had remedial classes for dyslexic children. As it happened, on the day of my visit a teacher was testing an eight-year-old girl who was a new student. Like me, she had red hair and was tall for her age; she reminded me of myself. Watching her perform, I saw for the first time how maddening it must be to be the parents or the teacher of a dyslexic child. The girl would puzzle over a word and then make a wild guess at it, or stand in silence for long periods, shifting from one foot to the other as she stared at the page, her thoughts obviously miles away. I realized why my teachers had become so impatient with me and why every reading lesson ended with me in tears and my teacher frustrated and angry.

The difference between that girl and me was that she didn't shed any tears. She wasn't even terribly uncomfortable about her failure to perform. Today people are more informed about dyslexia and are treating it in a more compassionate way. In my day a child who couldn't read was branded as stupid — an epithet that's hard to live with and hard to shake. Grown men and women who were early readers never lose the sense of intellectual superiority they felt as children, and those of us who couldn't read never lose our inferiority. Even a genius like W. B. Yeats, who couldn't learn to read, never entirely lost the scars on his psyche.

It wasn't easy for me to come out of the closet and write about being the class dunce. But doing it has been a tremendous satisfaction, because, of all the things I've written, *Reversals* is the book I've had the most mail about. I continue to hear from dyslexics who say that I told their story. They tell me about their built-in sense of shame — the feeling that they are defective — and about the ruses they still use to get along in a literate society. Recently I got a call from a woman in London who had read my book and realized for the first time that she was dyslexic. She's sixty years old and her children are grown and out of the house, and she wanted to know what she could do now to improve her limited ability to read — which she had concealed, or hoped she had concealed, even from her children.

With *Orphans* I suffered tremendous anxiety; it was by far the most emotionally demanding of my books. People often assume that writing a memoir is easy because you have all the material at hand. It's your personal history; you don't have to "create" or invent anything. That's true. What's *not* easy, at least for me, is to make that private history public.

In this case my editor wanted me to begin the book with the explosion of my feeling of being an orphan that followed the death of my second husband, Robert Simpson, when I was in my fifties. Until Bob died I had never felt like an orphan, in the sense of being really bereft. Bob's death very belatedly opened the whole subject, and I mourned for the first time for my parents, who died when I was a child — my mother when I was an infant and my father when I was seven. "That's the way the book has to start," my editor said. But when I tried to do that I got so anxious that I could hardly sit at the typewriter. I realized that I planned to put this material near the end of the book because I didn't want to examine what had happened.

So I decided to back into the book — a useful device, as I've found more than once. I would start by doing some research on how orphans have been treated historically. That would be easier than writing about my own childhood because it was more objective. Well, I went to the 42nd Street library and found some accounts of orphanages in and around New York from the 1880s to just before World War II, and I couldn't bear to read them. They had pictures of quite small, malnourished children standing over huge vats of laundry feeding sheets into a mangle, or eating their meager meals off a tin plate.

I was especially interested in the old Jewish orphanage on Amsterdam Avenue, a forbidding structure I used to pass as a child on my way to the dentist. I used to wish I could peek over the wall to see what went on there. Now I was finding out. That orphanage had kept pretty good records; it had a social worker who tracked down some former orphans to find out what their lives were like after they left. It was very sad; many of them lived in one furnished room and ate lonely meals at a cafeteria. The orphanage had so isolated them from the outside world that they were poorly prepared when they finally left. One of them remembered that at holiday time the orphans were invited to the homes of rich people, where they were given a lot of fine food and presents, so he assumed that that was how everybody lived and how he would live when he went out on his own.

After reading those accounts I would leave the library so gloomy that I'd say "I can't take any more of this." I'd stop, and for months I would find excuses not to return. Once it was almost a year before I went back to the book. But the subject wouldn't let go of me. So I backed up still farther. I decided to read autobiographies of writers who had been orphaned in their childhood — Rousseau, Sartre, Tolstoy. I got so caught up in Tolstoy's orphanhood that I thought, "This subject is so rich that I've got to do this book." Finally I finished my research and was able to start writing my own story.

At that moment I realized for the first time what a tremendous loss it had been not to have a mother. I had always said, "Oh, I didn't need a mother." Like Mary McCarthy, who lost both her parents when she was young and developed the same defense of denial, I had to say that I was so strong that I could get along without a mother. I had made a little scenario of my orphanhood that worked if no excessive burdens were put on it. Then Bob died and the whole thing collapsed. The reaction was just waiting for me. I suppose if my husband had outlived me I would never have had to face the earlier bereavements.

Was writing *Orphans* worth all that pain? I hope it was. I

certainly learned things about myself and about my child-hood that I hadn't known before — things I never could have learned just from research. I also hope the book has been helpful to other people who have been orphaned in one way or another. But after I finished it I said "Enough!" Whatever I might write in the future would be objective, external, outside myself. No more autobiography! No more memoir!

IAN FRAZIER

Looking for
My Family

My father became sick in about 1982 with Alzheimer's disease, and part of the difficulty was that for a long time we didn't know what was wrong with him. He finally died in 1987. My mother, who had most of the care of him, became sick right after he died, and she died the following year. These were quite sudden events, even though we expected my father's death, and they left my parents' apartment in chaos. My brother and my sisters and I had to clean it out, and as we did I found an enormous amount of family papers going back to previous generations. I told my brother and my sisters that I wanted those papers.

At first the papers were puzzling because they just looked like a big mess. But I had already looked at them enough to notice that there were letters that went back to 1855. I knew it was a trove of some kind. It was one of those situations where you either put it away and never look at it and feel guilty about it for the rest of your life and let your kids throw it away, or you do something about it. Luckily, it coincided with a perfect moment for me to embark on a project requiring that kind of intensive research. My daughter was born eleven weeks after my mother died, so we had a new baby and we were in this apartment in Brooklyn. My previous book, *Great Plains*, had been a rambling project that took me on many long drives out West. This new book called for a research method that fit with my new life at home. Just as you cook with what's in season, you write with what's most congenial to your life at that moment; you go with what your natural tendency is. My natural tendency just then was to be up at odd hours and to be sitting in my study.

So I started going through my parents' papers and objects, dividing them up. I made a box labeled "The Mom Museum" and another one called "The Dad Museum," in which I put all kinds of things pertaining to my parents — things that were evocative of them, like my dad's ties. He bought his ties in 1945 and could never see the point of changing them. Ties in 1945 were practically rectangular and about eleven inches long. My dad wore the same ties his entire life. Ties got thin, ties got fat, ties got thin again, ties got short, and he just wore the same ties from 1945 on. So I have those ties. And many other things. My dad was a chemist. So I have beakers. And safety glasses. He would hardly open a can without putting on his safety glasses, so I have his various safety glasses. I have all my mother's purses. My mother never threw away a purse — I have the history of purses back to 1942, in sequence.

I took all these things and went through them under a

light, almost with a magnifying glass, like a paleontologist inferring a culture or a species from a fragment of bone. I wanted to take my parents' lives as a piece to infer the culture they came from and its plot. I recorded each item in a notebook, as if I were cataloging something in a museum, identifying and describing each object. I read every one of those hundreds of letters and transcribed the important parts, because I knew from previous research how tough it is, once you've started to write and want to find something, to dig back through your files for it. It was easier just to copy the original letter.

Over the years I've done hundreds of hours of research in the New York Public Library. Often I'll come across a long passage that I want to have copied, and there's a long line of people waiting for the copying machine. So I think "I could stand in the line for two hours or I could copy this by hand in forty minutes," and I'll copy it right there in the Library, the way you see art students in the Metropolitan Museum copying paintings. If I were a writing teacher I'd have students copy stuff; it's a great way to really see the material. A lot of the charm of my parents' letters was the precise locution they had for certain things, and by copying those letters out I could preserve my parents' inflections. All that copying gave me easy reference points in my notebooks that I could turn to quickly, because the biggest bummer in nonfiction writing is when you need the reference and you're ripping through your notes, by the time you find it your mind is a hundred miles away from where it was. So I'm very proud of my notebooks.

As I said, the process meshed perfectly with my schedule of waking up to feed the baby and then being awake, or just having hours and hours when I don't know what I would have been doing otherwise. Previously, when I was writing *Great Plains*, I learned a lot about Indian arts. I really admire Native American handmade objects, like porcupine quillwork. As I looked at those objects in museums out West, I realized what frame of mind a person must have been in to do that kind of work. I realized that it was all done by women; the men were away, probably hunting or raiding, and the women were waiting. I felt that this was the same kind of a moment in my life. There are times when I'm able to study with great intensity and there are times when I can't. This was a time when I could.

My method in writing this memoir was to look for artifacts that suggested narrative. If you're going through letters, for example, the first thing you do is to date all the letters and put them in chronological order. That's your plot right there. In some cases I was really lucky. With my grandmother I had letters she wrote in 1939, when my mother first went away to school, and I had the last letter she wrote in her life, in 1961. I had the entire body. I could see her get well and get sick and get well and get sick and move to Arizona. I could see the plot of what happened to her.

Narrative is also suggested by physical objects — things like the programs of plays my mother was in as a girl. I could tell what every production meant to her, because the programs had connections to other objects in my Mom Museum, like congratulatory telegrams. My mother saved them all. Nobody sends telegrams anymore, but Western

Union used to have these beautiful telegram forms that were specifically designed for congratulations, with flowers on top, so it looked as if you were getting flowers. You've seen old movies where the leading lady is in her dressing room and there are Western Union telegrams everywhere. My mother got dozens of those telegrams when she was acting at the Lakewood Little Theater in Cleveland. I came upon thousands of objects like that, which told some kind of story, like my father's Navy ID cards. The question you ask is: What story does this object tell? Often I had to leave what I had at home and go to the public library, or go to the place where a particular event happened. To understand what you have in the way of ephemera you have to be ready to do a whole bunch of different things to invest them with meaning.

For instance, I made an angel food cake. My grandmother was famous for her angel food cakes. It's hard to make an angel food cake. My sister said, "Look, here's how she did it: She started with thirteen egg whites, which she would beat for some immense amount of time, and she'd do it on a flat plane; you can't use a mixer to do it properly." One of the many things I discovered by making that cake was how much more those people lived in terms of the weather than we do today. An angel food cake has to be made on the right day — you can't make it on a 100-percent-humidity day in the middle of July; it's just never going to happen. Then I realized that there were people whose birthday fell in one of those bad months. For those people my grandmother would work a heck of a lot harder to make a cake. In my book I talk a lot about the housekeeping tasks my grandmother did that most people today couldn't even identify. Doing some of those tasks made me understand her better and gave me an authority to write about her.

But none of my housekeeping experiments per se made it into the book. As a writer you have to have far more information than you finally use. I've read David Mamet's theories on acting, where the actor has an intention inside that he doesn't reveal. I've noticed, for instance, that if somebody tells a story and they know what the punch line is and they love the punch line, the story can be quite long, but their faith in the punch line invests each sentence with an immediacy that makes you think you're getting somewhere, and sometimes you reach the end and then there's no punch line at all. It's just the *idea* that there's a punch line. In my book that has a direct parallel with the notion of faith as it existed in the culture that my family came out of — the notion that if you believe something it invests everything you do with meaning.

The culture I'm talking about is American Protestant culture — the original force of conviction that motivated someone like Stonewall Jackson, whom I describe at length in the book. Because of the strength of Jackson's faith and the years he had invested in figuring out what it was, he could tell you a fact or give an order and it meant something. It was strong. Yet if you were to say to him, "Look, what exactly do you believe?" you might completely disagree with what he says or have a hundred objections to it, but it wouldn't matter because his secular personality makes use of it in a way that he doesn't reveal. What I'm saying is, if you know where you're going as a writer and you have faith in where you're going, it makes each sentence seem to say, "This must be going some-where." If you *don't* know, it pulls the rug out from under each sentence. Suddenly the reader says, "Wait a minute — he doesn't know where he's going. Let's stop and navi-gate here, because we're lost." That's where you're going to lose the reader.

Of course there comes a time when you have to stop the research and start writing. I did as much research as I could imagine I would need, over two and a half years. Research is a siren — you find one thing, and you find the next thing, and then you find the next thing. When I was work-ing on the religion chapter in *Family* I was reading books on religion. I read one by Harold Bloom. I had never read anything by him before, and I said, "My God, this guy's great — I should read everything by Harold Bloom." Then I looked at the list of all his books and I said, "No, read *one book* only by Harold Bloom or you'll die." His *The American Religion* is a really interesting book, and it's also a wacky book — he'll try a wacky theory on you and stand behind it with a lot of guts, and it really made me think. But I had to stop myself at that point.

It's like building a house. You get to a certain part and you realize that you need a different gauge of lumber or something, and you have to go get it. For example, I love the Civil War and I know a fair amount about it. I love American frontier history and I know a lot about that. But

I discovered that I had one big blank spot, between 1865 and 1920. I thought I had the period covered in the chapter about my great grandfather, Louis Wickham, whom I actually knew. He was a self-documenting person, and I had a lot of stuff about him. He was born in 1866 in Norwalk, Ohio, a town his ancestors had founded, and he became a small-town lawyer. I assumed that he would take me through that era, and one day I realized that he wasn't going to. So I had to take three or four months out of the middle of my writing and go to the New York Public Library and just read about his period.

I began by reading Arthur Schlesinger, Sr., who was an interesting historian. He wrote a very large book, *The Rise of the City*, about America in the years from about 1875 to 1915, and it had a lot of sources and notes. I dug into those notes, and then I went from the notes to other sources. I went to Ohio and read newspapers from those years. That opened up the whole period for me: its revivalism and corruption and spiritual confusion and repression; and its resistance to ideas, ranging from new discoveries in geology to Biblical scholarship; and, above all, the rise of the Prohibition movement, which I thought was the biggest mistake the Protestant establishment ever made. I saw how the idea of Prohibition spread through the culture, using a lot of the energy that was left over from abolition. That was fascinating to me because much of my book takes place in the Western Reserve in northeastern Ohio, a fifty-mile-wide strip in which the Women's Christian Temperance Union and the Sons of Temperance and the Anti-Saloon League all began. Later, Alcoholics Anonymous was born in nearby Akron. So that was a rich subplot that I hadn't known about.

When I began writing *Family* I knew it would be nonfiction but I didn't know exactly what its genre would be. As it turned out, I was writing a compendium of nonfiction styles. I love all different kinds of nonfiction styles. I like history. I like technical writing. I like science description. I like memoir. I like first-person narrative. But whatever my style, the main strain that emerged was a family history. Which can be a very boring kind of book, where somebody just goes on and on about all the people he or she is related to. The artist Saul Steinberg once told me that I write fake boring books — books that you think would be boring, but then they're not. Faux boring. I tried to make this book sneakily interesting. I've always been willing to go in some off-the-wall direction — to drop everything and just run with it, where other writers might think, "I can't disrupt the fabric of my narrative." Ideally, each veer will make the narrative less boring.

That tendency of mine is a direct result of bouncing off William Shawn in the years when he was editor of *The New Yorker* and I was writing articles for him. It grew out of knowing what Shawn's threshold of boredom was. I would see his comments in the margins of my articles saying, "There's no reason for this part of the piece at all." Rick Hertzberg once wrote a wonderful profile of a guy who was a minor-league baseball club owner. The guy goes to a bar and meets someone who says he has the biggest ranch in Texas. The guy doesn't believe him, and he takes him out to his ranch, and the ranch has millions of goats, and there's this long digression where everybody is driving around the prairie drunk in the middle of the morning. Shawn wrote in the margins, "This is neither funny nor interesting," and the section came out. My objective in dealing with Shawn was to tease him into keeping a section like that — to get him to say, "Well, it's not funny or interesting, but OK." I find the analogy of the courtroom helpful in writing. A trial lawyer veers off on something and the other lawyer cries "Objection! Objection!" and "That's immaterial!" As a writer you want to plant certain notions in the reader's mind, just as the lawyer wants to plant them in the jury's mind. I've often found, when people have read one of my pieces, that they will refer to something that was at first glance immaterial to the article. That was the one thing that stayed with them. Your objective is to find something that corresponds with the reader — something he or she has an affinity for, or can understand. It's a seduction. The reader thinks he knows what he wants, and if you can just tease him away from that he'll often have a better time than he would have had going where he thought he wanted to go.

From the start of writing *Family* I needed to know that I had a plot. My plot was the disintegration of the Protestant establishment. Now, to come right out and say that might make the book sound less interesting to someone who didn't know that that's what the plot was. But if I hadn't had that theme to lean back on, to sustain me, the book would have been like marbles spilled across the floor.

All families spill and scatter and disintegrate; in many ways it's as hard to write about them as it is to fit a family tree onto a single sheet of paper. One thing I regret not doing in this book was to add a disclaimer to help the reader, like "*I* can't follow these people. The great-great-grandfather confuses *me*. He'll confuse *you*. Don't worry about the math of it — hooking everybody up, figuring out who's who. The point is the sense of these people and the sense of their lives, not who was my great-grandfather on my mother's side."

A parallel plot of the book is the attempt to give meaning to my parents' lives. The two plots — their story and the Protestant decline — coincide at the point of the death of my parents and the earlier death of my brother. A hundred years ago, before the Protestant enterprise hopped the rails, people would have known how to deal with those tragedies. For instance, my parents never said anything to anybody about what my brother's death meant to them; it wasn't integrated into any view of what life is about. Americans in their day had less cultural unity — fewer immune systems — to fight off this kind of tragedy than people had in the nineteenth century. Children then died far more often, and parents knew they had to find a way to contend with it or it could destroy their life; everybody couldn't die when kids die, because kids died all the time.

So it struck me that one of the meanings of my parents' lives was how they reacted to this disintegration of religious values. They always had wine with their dinner. In the previous generation, especially in that part of the country, if you gave people wine they might well have been offended; their custom was to say grace before dinner. But my parents had wine and gave a toast. They did it because when they were kids they sat through a lot of graces; they were making a statement. Protestantism can be a gloomy situation if you get into it too deep, and they wanted out of that — they wanted to enjoy life. And the successful people of that generation *did* enjoy life; the Prohibitionists died a grim death, basically. So that's one point where my two plots coincide.

I grew up in a suburban development, so this is also a book about the suburbs. One of the meanings I found as I wrote the book was the aridity of what had at first seemed a dream way to grow up. But it turns out that the theory of the suburbs wasn't good. I saw that it was basically racist and consumerist. It was also horribly reductive, because each house became its own little place. Connections were shattered; the nuclear family became the only family, whereas previously, in a small town or in a city neighborhood, you had an extended family. I was surprised to discover how explicitly the suburbs had been established as a one-race community. I guess I knew that in my bones, but I really found it out by writing the book.

One great thing about this kind of eclectic research is that you come across wonderful books, like *Crabgrass Frontier*, by Kenneth T. Jackson. That book taught me about where I had grown up. You live in a place with an immense history, but each generation parcels out that history as it sees fit. Nobody ever told me that the abolitionist John Brown lived in my hometown of Hudson, Ohio, from the age of five until he was twenty, that he raised money for his raids in Kansas there, or that he spoke in the chapel of the school where I went to high school. I had to learn all that in my research, and it made for an interesting continuum — that the town went from abolitionist stronghold to exclusionary suburb.

Looking at the history of my town made me curious in turn about the settlement of America. I read the entire *History of France and England in the New World* by Francis Parkman — all ten volumes. Parkman's prejudice is that Catholicism was basically wrong for the job of settling the new world; he makes the Catholic countries of France and Spain seem inefficient compared with Protestant England. Extending this idea, I came to the conclusion that sectarian Protestants were far more adaptable to spreading out and covering a big and varied landscape because of their tendency to keep dividing. I came upon hundreds of names of Protestant sects that I had never heard of: Winebrennerites and Zoarites and Schwenck-felders. There were Hooker Mennonites, who fastened their clothes with hooks, and Button Mennonites, who used buttons. I began to notice a similarity to Native American culture, because when I had finished my research for *Great Plains* I was practically drowning in the names of Indian tribes. Indians settled this continent efficiently. They didn't *hold* it efficiently, but they settled it efficiently by moving into all these varied places. How did they do it? By dividing. How did the Protestants do it? By dividing.

Once the Protestant movement lost its fire, once the

tide had crested and begun to fall back, it created the suburb as a small exclusionary settlement. At first the small-town Protestants went to the cities, but they couldn't stand the cities because they were small-town people, so they came back and created these communities that were half city, half small town. Reading about that historic process gave me a way of explaining the suburbs to myself, finding out where I had come from. Once I feel grounded in history I'm so much more comfortable as a writer. I'm far more comfortable in my hometown now than I was when I was growing up there. In theory, suburbia was the place where people moved to have kids. But the sad punch line was, "When you're not a kid anymore, get out. Or get kids of your own." Well, in suburbs like the one where I grew up, you're not going to have the money to buy a house until you're in your thirties. So there's a very shaky period, between age eighteen and the time you get married and have kids and do have money to buy a house (assuming you have that much success), when you're adrift. Understanding all that has been one of the rewards of writing my book.

Altogether, as I said, I spent two and a half years doing research for *Family* and another two and a half years writing it. Shaping that much material can be daunting. I began with the premise that I wanted to get at least one thing right. My analogy comes from hunting. When you're in a field and a whole bunch of quail go up, if you're a beginner you put your gun to your shoulder and just go BANG. You see all those birds and you shoot at them all and you won't get one. If you want to get a bird, pick *one* bird and shoot it. I've seen films of wolves pursuing a herd of caribou. They will pick one out. The wolf will run into a herd of thousands and will chase that one caribou through the herd — and get it.

So, first, get one thing right — one thing that you really want to say. Once you get it right, look at it and see what it implies, because that one detail or observation that seems so beautiful to you can often point to narrative. It can be the first step in a sequence of equally evocative details. It's like a seed crystal; you can build on it, even if it's just one sentence. Some nonfiction books are built on a single sentence. The writer Alex Shoumatoff once told me about the Colorado River. He said that because of irrigation and dams and aridity, not a drop of that mighty river reaches the ocean. To me that's an excellent fact to build a whole book on. When I did my research for *Family* I was reading about turkey shoots on the frontier. The men would pen a turkey behind a log and shoot at its head, and if you shot its head off you won the turkey. But a hit on the bird's bill didn't count. I wanted to put that fact in — it meant an enormous amount to me. I told other people about it, and it meant more to me than it did to anyone else, but to me it's a very funny fact, because of course it counted to the bird — to get its bill shot off.

I came to this notion from writing humor. I began my career as a humor writer, doing short magazine pieces. In a humor piece, if you think something is really funny, if it corresponds to something in your heart that you really care about and love, if it's not in there when you're finished, you didn't write a good piece. The same is true of writing a book. If the part you love is not there, it doesn't matter how much else you did. I've witnessed battles between writers and editors that you can't believe the intensity of. But the writer knows that if that point came out, the book wouldn't be his.

When I was working on this book, people sometimes said, "*I've* got all this family stuff too, and I'd like to write it, but I'm afraid of what my family would say." There's no escaping that — guilt is the headwind that you sail into. It's incredibly strong. In my case it was so strong that I did extreme things to combat it. But you *can* combat it — give all your money to charity, or whatever makes you feel less guilty, and then you can work, because the reader doesn't care how guilty you feel. Guilt is a form of narcissism. I told almost everybody who is in my book what I wrote about them; I asked their permission. My goal was not to reveal what a jerk Uncle Roy was — this isn't investigative reporting. Generally I don't write about things I don't love. Still, love of the subject didn't take the guilt away, because first you have plain old survivor's guilt; you're writing about the dead. If somebody had said to my great-grandfather, pointing to me, "This little kid with his baseball cap on backwards is going to tell a lot of people what your life meant, he's going to be the sole repository of your good name," he might have been outraged. I also felt uneasy writing about the Civil War veterans, because of how much that war was a part of their life and how much they cared about it. I knew I wasn't going to get it completely right, and I felt the weight of their invisible displeasure.

It's psychic jujitsu that you have to do — you have to throw all those fears and misgivings before you can write. I know many people with incredible family histories, and often the more incredible those stories are, the more guilt-inducing they are. I was lucky that I didn't have to write around any shameful thing in my family. There was the average good-and-evil battle, but I didn't have something horrible to avoid or to deal with. But all these decisions precede writing. If you can't deal with them you won't be able to write your book. I just kept dosing my guilt with one thing or another to reduce it to a size I could live with. I recommend that to memoir writers: Make a nice dinner for everybody — something that makes you feel you've done good for someone. Fortunately, most people do want to be written about. They want their lives to be known and remembered. They may be wary when you describe your project to them, especially if you look like some kind of loose cannon. But once it's done they're usually happy.

HENRY LOUIS GATES, JR.

Lifting the Veil

I wrote *Colored People* because I was grieving for my mother. She died in April, 1977, and contrary to what most people say about grief, mine dissipated very slowly. It was a long time before I could get out of bed and walk around and get back to my work without feeling paralyzed or totally preoccupied.

At that time my two daughters were five and seven years old. As they got older and as I got older I developed more understanding for the person my mother had been in middle age, before she went through the menopause that abruptly changed her whole life. It was only as *I* approached middle age that I began to think about her trauma in a systematic way. I found myself intensely missing the person she once was. At the same time, I realized that my daughters had no more idea of who *I* was — what my life was like — than the man in the moon.

So those were the motivations that went into my memoir. Essentially, it was a relationship with someone in the generation before me. I wanted to retrieve a narrative from all that pain of my mother's, not only for myself but for her female descendants — my daughters. One of them looks just like her and one of them acts just like her, and neither of them knows anything about her because they were only five and seven when she died.

I had so many vivid memories of that earlier period. My father is still living, and he's a great storyteller. Every family has its canonical tales, and I've been hearing many of the stories that went into this book all my conscious life. So I wanted to create a portrait of my mother — for my mother, for myself, and for my daughters — in my father's vernacular voice, while my father was still living.

My brother is a prominent oral surgeon at a New York hospital. At the beginning of my career I wrote a lot of deconstructionist and post-structuralist criticism. But I was always a literary journalist, and I prided myself on being able to write accessibly. I wanted to be Edmund Wilson, not Jacques Derrida. But even when I published a review in, say, the *New York Times*, my brother and his friends, who belonged to book clubs and were lawyers and doctors and dentists, couldn't understand what I meant. The joke was — and it was always a twist, you knew the knife was turning — when are you going to write a book that Mama and Daddy can read? So I wanted to be able to fulfill that challenge from my brother.

In the summer of 1992 I had just finished my first year as a professor at Harvard, and I had a fellowship to go to Bellagio, the Rockefeller Foundation's center on Lake

Como, near Milan. I had justified the application in some bullshit way: I was going to write an introduction to the complete essays of Zora Neale Hurston. It had to be something you could do in six weeks. So what can you do in six weeks? You can write an introduction.

I got to Bellagio late at night, in a heavy fog. But even through the fog I realized that this was an amazing place. It was like a castle. The next morning I woke up around six and my room was dark. It had big steel shutters, and I went over and finally figured out how to open them, and it was like when you used to watch *Walt Disney Presents* on TV on Sunday night: the screen would dissolve and it was fantasy land. It was the most beautiful view I had ever seen. There was a beautiful mountain and a beautiful lake and you could see vineyards and greenhouses and servants working. It was so beautiful that I got all excited and got a burst of energy. I went down for breakfast and the director said, "Every scholar here has his own study and yours is the *Veduta*, which means view. It's up on the hill outside the villa. It's called the *Veduta* because it has three windows and there's a view of the lake from each of the windows. It's shaped like a silo so that you can have a circular desk and put chairs in front of each window and follow the sun."

Well, as they were walking me up to this fantasy study I looked out on the lake and I remembered a day when my Uncle Nemo took me fishing. There was something about the way this all looked that reminded me of that event. So I sat down and wrote a letter to my daughters, Maggie and Liza. I wrote: "July 11th — Dear Maggie and Liza, I'm sitting in a silo-shaped study called the *Veduta*, which means the view in Italian. And walking up here reminded me of the time Uncle Nemo . . . You didn't know Uncle Nemo — he died and he was Mama's brother." That's how I started.

Piedmont, where I grew up in West Virginia, is on the Potomac River in the Allegheny Mountains, so it's a stretch to say that Bellagio reminded me of the Allegheny Mountains, but it did. Today when I see Piedmont it looks like Bellagio, but not to anybody else. Bellagio was a mnemonic device — the place reminded me so much of growing up. Several friends of mine who are writers and editors had been telling me, "You should write a memoir," because I always put these anecdotes in my essays, and a lot of them are really funny — they're mostly my father's stories. So every day for the next two weeks at Bellagio I wrote twenty to thirty pages in the form of a letter to my daughters, and it just flowed. It was a miracle. I knew I was on to something good. I would Xerox all the pages — I wrote in longhand on legal pads — and I'd FedEx the originals to my secretary back at Harvard, and she would type them. I went to Milan and bought some new clothes and came back and wrote for two more weeks. And that was it — that was the first draft of the book. I've never written anything that fast before.

When I got back to Harvard the whole manuscript was there in the form of a long letter. Two of my friends, who had been reading over my secretary's shoulder, said, "It's raw and it needs editing, but it's great." So I sent it to Knopf, where I was under contract to do three books, and they said they liked it. But it was very raw. I had made myself extremely vulnerable — I talked a lot about my sexuality and my loves and my hates. I sent it to several friends whose judgment I trust, and they said, "In six months you won't want to have it published." They also said, "Because it's in the form of letters to your daughters, and your daughters are too young, it shouldn't be left in this epistolary form." The writing had been such an intense experience that I needed a few months to think about it.

But then I knew that my friends were right. So I rewrote the whole book in a prose style; all that's left of the letter to Maggie and Liza is the preface. I also cut down on some things I thought would be better left undisclosed. This time I tried to write in my father's voice. A lot of the passages with no quotation marks are clearly mimicking a black voice — my father's. His friends and my relatives and brothers said, "You got Daddy's voice absolutely right." Of course it's also my voice — I use a black vernacular when I tell stories; I slip into it effortlessly. Still, in this case it's more a matter of me imitating my father's voice. They're his stories.

The lesson for me in writing *Colored People* is that if you're going to tell the truth, that determines what kind of memoir you'll do. I told myself I was writing a memoir about a particular time and place. I was on the eve of my forty-second birthday when I wrote it — too young to write an autobiography; this isn't the story of how I became XYZ. Ostensibly I was writing a memoir about a lost time and place — a lost mother, an aging father, a dying town — and I had the device of the letters to my daughters to justify it. But when I started writing, it turned out to be not only this one small window on my past; it was everything. I was peeling away all these layers of memory about my relationship to my parents. Previously, I hadn't been in therapy. But as soon as I finished writing the book I realized that I needed to talk to a therapist. As it turned out, that therapy brought back a crucial event that I had completely repressed — the day they took my mother to the hospital and I thought I had been responsible for her illness by crossing my legs in a certain way. That incident explained everything: why I joined the church and why I always felt such a strong sense of guilt. The book was virtually in galleys when I recovered that memory, but I knew I had to insert it. Writing that episode was agony — dealing with something buried so deep that suddenly had come to the surface.

Of course the act of writing is more important than the therapy. But my advice to anybody writing a memoir is: Be prepared for the revelation of things you don't even dream are going to come up. My other advice is: Don't sit around and wait until you have the story; just start telling the story. That's what my writing teachers always said, but I never did it before. This book wrote itself. I would look at my pen and think, "This is the smartest pen in all of Italy." It was easy because I was away from home. I didn't have phones or faxes unless I wanted them, and I had a story to tell.

The danger is self-indulgence. When you write an auto-biography or a memoir you're indulging yourself in your own sentimentality. So I found ways to guard against that:

by using irony and wit and self-deprecation, and also by being honest, or revelatory, about pain and fear. Those are the techniques of a craftsman, but they're important because a memoir is all about the unfolding of your ego, and you need to deflect your presence. You're center stage but you need to move yourself to the periphery.

One of the decisions that had to be made when I rewrote *Colored People*, taking it out of the epistolary form, was how to give it some kind of shape. Chronology is always useful, and my book is more or less chronological. But I also divided it into certain motifs, like the chapter about hair, "In the Kitchen," which describes in detail how Mama used to do hair with a "hot comb." A lot of people have said, "Did you fear that this was a risk: that you were lifting the family veil and telling family secrets — not only literally family secrets but, metaphorically, family secrets and racial secrets and ethnic secrets?" The answer is yes. But I wasn't any more honest about our culture or about my mother's family than I was about myself. That was important to me. I took myself as the bottom line. I think mine is the first generation of black people in America who can afford to be this open.

I wanted to write a book that imitated the specialness of black culture when no white people are around. Older black people don't talk a certain way when white people are around; they're never ultimately comfortable. I could be blindfolded and know whether a white person was in the room. Sometimes it's the nuance of thought; sometimes it's the accent; sometimes it's whether the "ings" are

pronounced; sometimes it's how much vulgarity or vernacular is being used. Generally, for instance, black people
don't talk about white people, or white racism. It may
come up, but you're talking about all kinds of stuff. If you
read black literature you'd think the only thing black people talk about is white people and white racism, which is
just not true. They're concerned about who's screwing
whom, and about their jobs, and about what everybody's
afraid of — love and death, the great themes.

So I wanted to write a book that was honest in that way,
that imitated what it might be like if you were a microphone or a videocamera on the sofa in our living room
circa 1955 and 1965, without the racial thought police or
racial censors interrupting the flow. The same way that if
somebody came into the room and tried to tell my father
that *Amos 'n' Andy* wasn't funny and he shouldn't watch it,
he would have told him to get out of his house. Or if
someone had said the use of the word "motherfucker" is
inappropriate he would have said, "Motherfucker! Get the
motherfuck out of my house!" That's what I wanted to do.
That's the black culture that I love.

When I'm with my friends, no matter how successful or
how integrated we might be today, when we're by ourselves we talk that stuff. We tell those stories. I wanted my
book to be one of the first books that crossed that line, and
I was willing to take that risk. I said, "Look, some people
aren't going to like it, no matter what I do. But it's *my*
book." Actually this is my fourth book. The first two I had
to write to get tenure. The third book, *Loose Canons*, which
I enjoyed writing, was a collection of essays on the literary

canon wars. But in a way I feel that this is my first book. It's belletristic. It's a trade book. And it's for me. You only pass through once.

In most of the homes of people I know I'm surrounded by books. But if you look at how many of those books are autobiographies of women or people of color, just by definition there won't be that many. I think it's important that the particularity of those life experiences be registered with as much frequency as the life stories of white men. We used to think that in order to write you had to be James Baldwin or W. E. B. DuBois or Frederick Douglass or Richard Wright — a bona fide author, someone special. But one of the great benefits of the explosion of writing by black women today is that more and more "ordinary" people are telling their story — because, by telling your own history, if you're a member of a historically oppressed or narratively excluded group, you can tell a new collective history through each of these books. This is a chapter of the larger narrative of the Negro in America.

Whatever your group, write, write, and keep writing. If you are Puerto Rican, Chicano, a woman, an African-American woman, an African-American man, gay — keep writing. Many gay people have written their autobiography over the centuries, but very few of those gay establishment people wrote about being gay. Today the challenge is to make gayness one of the levels of storytelling. In my case, for instance, my evolution in consciousness about being black in the world is my first thematic level. My coming to sexuality is another level. My relationship to my parents is another — there are many levels. I think it's very important for people in marginalized groups to tell multilayered stories that address the problems of their oppression — a gay person writing about what it's like to be gay — but that also let a reader know that even for a gay person who feels under siege, being gay is not all they think about all day long. Their story has to be something that works like art. It has to work on several narrative levels.

*

Q. An important passage in *Colored People*, I think, is the one in which you describe how the colored community of Piedmont had its particular world in order and didn't want it to be shaken by upstarts like you:

> The soul of that world was colored. Its inhabitants went to colored schools, they went to colored churches, they lived in colored neighborhoods, they ate colored food, they listened to colored music, and when all that fat and grease finally closed down their arteries or made their hearts explode, they slept in colored cemeteries, escorted by colored preachers: old black-suited southern preachers, with shiny black foreheads and an insatiable desire for fried chicken, men for whom preaching is a personal call from God, a direct line on His cellular telephone. They dated colored, married colored, divorced and cheated on colored. And when they could, they taught at colored colleges, preached to colored congregations, trimmed nappy hair on colored heads, and, after the fifties, even fought to keep alive the tradi-

tion of the segregated all-colored schools. They feared that world where so much humiliation had lain in wait, ambushing them blindsided, unawares. And they hated that which made them fear. That is, I think, why they hated some of us, the first generation of integrated wannabes, recognizing us as the real threat to the ordered universe they had constructed with such painstaking care for such a long time. It was like hoeing an acre of drought-stricken land with a wooden stick, Uncle Jim told me one day, out in the fishing boat, referring to their efforts to purchase the houses where they now lived.

As a member of that first generation, were you consciously trying to write one of the first books that would be a symbol of a new authenticity for other black people to emulate?

One of the things I had to decide between the first and second draft of *Colored People* was how revelatory I wanted to be. In my generation, if *I* can't do it, who can? I'm a very secure and successful person in my own little sphere (knock on wood); I've been very lucky. And what's the point of achieving that success if you can't write about it? I love writing; I have for a long time. So I wanted to write something that I thought was beautiful and well crafted. But I also wanted to write something that made a difference to the African-American tradition that I teach. So I regard my book as a pivotal document in the formal development of memoir and autobiography in the African-

American tradition. I wanted to try to register a new voice and a new way of seeing — to make a departure. I didn't know how it would be received. I knew that some people wouldn't like it. I was surprised that as many people liked it as did — especially black reviewers. But I also knew that some black people would feel that I had lifted the veil too soon. Sometimes you get black people sitting around in a room and they'll say, "We can't afford to let The Man know this *yet.*" The "yet" connotes time — the time when we're secure enough as a people, when a white racist won't use a book that we've written against us. That's totally bogus. It's a totally unjustified claim to the need for black writers to censor themselves.

Richard Wright and James Baldwin never wrote one thing that got published without a white reader sitting on their shoulders, looking at what they wrote. They always had to worry about the lowest common denominator of white racism. That tradition was established in the eighteenth century, when Phillis Wheatley became the first black person to publish a book of poetry in English, because black writing had never previously been taken as literature. It was like the perennial IQ debate and what it implies about the native intelligence of the African and his or her fitness to be more than a slave. In the nineteenth century the argument became somewhat more refined, but not by much. Frederick Douglass and other slave narrators were all written about in this patronizing way: What does this mean about how soon we should let them be free? What does it mean about their status in the great chain of being? Are they really human beings? Did we all come from Adam and Eve? Do we constitute a separate species? All kinds of craziness. So those people never could have published a book like mine. It would have fed all the wrong things — the opinions not only of people who were vaguely racist, sitting in an apartment in New York, but of people who were in control of the fate of the race. All too often the writings of a person of African descent could be entered as anthropological evidence in a court or in a Supreme Court decision. It was almost as if black people were Martians, and to figure them out the white rulers had to examine every specimen of their minds, if indeed they had minds.

The rhetoric is so bizarre that it sounds hyperbolic of me to say it. But that's the way it is — the reality is much more hyperbolic than my language. That's still the legacy that all black writers have to contend with. You can see it in the critical reception by black men to Ntozake Shange's *For Colored Girls Who Have Considered Suicide When the Rainbow Is Enuf* and Alice Walker's *The Color Purple* and Toni Morrison's work. Many black men like Ishmael Reed and Stanley Crouch have written essays that say, "What will white racists think of black men if Alice Walker dares to depict a black man as evil and as sexist and as brutal as Mister in *The Color Purple*?" So when I teach *The Color Purple* I tell my students, "If you're a white racist you don't need Alice Walker. You're going to be a white racist no matter what."

This is the internal censor that black writers have always lived with. By internal I don't mean individual internal (though it is internalized that way), but ethnically internalized, because it has been internalized within the culture. I've only met a few successful black people who talk the same way around white people and black people: Vernon Jordan, say, or Quincy Jones, or Marion Wright Edelman. Vernon Jordan is one of the great storytellers; he tells the same jokes around white people and black people. But most black people will edit themselves for their audience. They'll say, "I shouldn't." They'll ask, "How will my story be appropriated against the race?"

In my memoir I pretended that I was sitting in my living room, writing down my father's stories. That was the device I used. I pretended that I was writing a book for my daughters about my mother, in my father's voice. That way I wouldn't betray my father's language. I love his language; I think it's very poetic. If I had imagined that I was writing for middle-class black ladies with white gloves on, I couldn't have written this book. I got a taste of how they would have reacted last year after the Oxford book on multiculturalism, which I edited, was published. I was asked to attend one of those events at the Waldorf — five hundred people with white gloves — and I decided to read the first draft of what became a chapter about my Uncle Nemo in *Colored People*. I said, "I know you want to hear about multiculturalism and I'll answer questions about that later, but I've just written this new book that I'm very excited about and I want to try it out. So first I'm going to tell you about my Uncle Jim." I read that episode, and it was about thunder thighs and getting nooky and stuff like that.

Afterward many black people in the audience came up to ask me to autograph my books. They clearly hadn't enjoyed what I had read. One woman said, "Professor Gates, I've always admired you, but you embarrassed our people today." So I knew that kind of reaction was out there; I had tried to share my book with an integrated audience, and their reaction really hurt my feelings. Later I read it to a black audience and they laughed hysterically. I realized that this middle-class black woman was embarrassed at being at the Waldorf with these white folks, wanting to hear some high rhetoric about multiculturalism and how we have to bring Cleopatra into the race and not have some black man talk about getting laid.

But I decided that it was time to tell the African-American story honestly. Each generation between Frederick Douglass and our generation has felt looser, I think, but Richard Wright and Ralph Ellison hated Zora Neale Hurston. She lifted the veil too much. Zora Neale Hurston only emerged as a great author of the black tradition when black women like Alice Walker brought her into the canon in the past fifteen years. Her books had gone out of print; she had been vilified and crushed by reviews by black writers who said, "You've revealed too much about darkies having a good time and getting laid and drinking wine." Richard Wright, in his review of Hurston in 1937, said that it was too much darkies singing songs out in the field and that it would confirm the worst expectations of white racism. I wanted to try to reverse that kind of critical reception, which is still repeated when black men review the writings of black women.

Today the black women writers are far ahead of the men. Someone once wrote an essay on black criticism called "In the Space Where Sex Should Be." The point was that in the space where sex should be, in the writings of black men like Baldwin and Wright and Ellison, is a white male who epitomizes white racism. Black men emerge by defeating white men rather than by talking about intimacy, or about consummation of sexual relations. Think about it: in all of *Native Son* or *Invisible Man* there's no healthy sex. When you're an adolescent, all you think about is sex, but you wouldn't know it from these books. Bigger Thomas in *Native Son* beats up Bessie and throws her down a shaft, but Bigger as a sexual being doesn't exist. He's a brute. Sexuality exists only so that Bigger can manifest another aspect of his own brutality, which in *Native Son* is produced by a racist, capitalist system. It was only when black women started writing that we got sex.

I don't know what the legacy of my book *Colored People* will be. If you ask me what I would like it to be, I would like it to make younger people feel freer to tell their own stories. And I would hope that the internal cultural censor is dead. To me it was like the black inquisition.

JILL KER CONWAY

Points of Departure

The motivations for writing *The Road from Coorain* were very complex. I'll start with the most frivolous and proceed to the most profound.

The most frivolous one was that after about the five-hundredth time some American or Canadian told me how much they loved the movie *Crocodile Dundee* I couldn't stand it any more, because that film is the most vulgar projection of an Australian male myth, packaged deliberately to appeal to American stereotypes. It has almost nothing to do with what life in the Australian outback is like. I grew up as a child with all those rootless, itinerant males, whose lives were mostly tragic and whose inability to connect to other people made them not the type of heroic natural man that Crocodile Dundee is presented as, but very pathetic figures. I was also tired to death of the obsessive re-creation of the male myth that we see traditionally in Australian movies, whether it's *Breaker Morant* or *Gal-*

lipoli or *The Man from Snowy River* — all of them about unattached males. Women are presented as a good lay on the way to the war, or something like that; they have no real existence. So I wanted to write a story about the Australian outback that has a female heroine — my mother — and a female narrative voice.

The second motivation is more complex. I used to write a great deal when I was young, before I got a Ph.D. As an undergraduate in Australia I loved to write. I published a number of books and articles, including a book for children. Later, at Harvard, working on my doctorate made me have difficulty writing. As an academic you internalize the critical voice of your supervisor and your fellow students and you lose access to spontaneous narrative. You begin to write for other historians and less and less from your own experience. Then I became a university administrator, first as vice president of the University of Toronto and then as president of Smith College. In that kind of position you write endless reams of memoranda to the board of trustees and goodness knows what other officialdom, and in all your communications there's always the legal department looking over your shoulder and fussing about language. You begin to write like a bureaucrat.

When I took the job at Smith I promised myself that I would only be a college president for ten years, because then I would be fifty and it would be time to get back to the writing I wanted to do. In the course of being a college president I started talking to other audiences — to alumni, or corporation executives, or testifying before congressional committees — so the range of people I was talking to and the audience I thought about became much broader. Still, when I sat down to write again after I left Smith, I just couldn't get away from that wretched bureaucratic prose. Once you've got the voice of authority and caution, it's very hard to get away from it. So I thought, "I'm going to have to write something that's really close to the bone and see if I can rediscover my own style."

The other motivations were much larger and ongoing in my life. I was interested in seeing if I could come up with a life plot that wasn't a romance, because the archetypal life plot for women in Western society is the bourgeois romance. It's about family and erotic life, and it doesn't concern itself at all with motivations that I think are very important for women, like work and intellectual life and political commitments. But I didn't want to write an odyssey — to just take over the archetypal male plot and create a conquering heroine. I was looking for a way to narrate a life story of a woman that would pay due respect to her attachments to men and to family but would be about something else entirely. I wanted to convey my sense of my education, of my liberation through access to education, and of the variety of steps by which I arrived at taking charge of my own life. Philosophically, you only have to perform one free act to be a free person. Granting all the ways in which we're shaped by society, nevertheless one free choice changes the outcome.

So I deliberately ended the *The Road from Coorain* with my departure from Australia, because that leaves the end totally open. Afterward people kept writing to me and saying, "I want to know what happened next." I could have ended the book two years later in the United States, when I married the man to whom I've been married for thirty-three years, and then everybody would have said, "Oh, so that's how it ended!" But it's very deliberately not a romance, and it's not an odyssey. I think of it as a quest narrative. That's appropriate for any life stage, because the modern consciousness, which separates some private essence that we think we have from the roles we play, leaves a thoughtful person with a quest to put all those lives together and see what they have added up to.

I also wanted — another motivation — to tell the story of my separation from my family, because when I became president of Smith and had office hours every Monday, at which anybody could come in and see me — the grounds-keeper or someone complaining that the basketball coach only played her two minutes last week — I found that the most recurring visits were from juniors and seniors who were overwhelmed by a sense of obligation to their families. They didn't feel entitled to a private destiny, and they were terribly conflicted about their sense of their true vocation and their duty to their family. Of course young men also have those feelings, but they have access to far more narratives about how one overcomes those crippling obligations. So I thought: Since this seems to be a universal problem and is unchanged for all ten generations of students I talked to at Smith, it's probably a very important theme.

Traditionally there has only been one female autobiography for every eight written by a male. And the romantic plot has so dominated the way women write their narratives that, to the extent that these women's books exist at all, they obscure how the woman chose to make her life. Jane Addams, my great heroine, who spent nine years founding Hull House, the great settlement house in Chicago, says in her autobiography that it would be hard to say when the idea of founding Hull House came into her mind, but it was probably when she was taken — just as a passive passenger — by a philanthropic worker to see the poor scrambling for food in the East End of London. I know from reading her diaries and letters that she bugged that woman to take her to the East End of London; she made it happen. But she never assumes responsibility.

Once I picked up that theme in her language I began to pay attention to it in other life narratives of women. By contrast, among males the sense of being the agent of one's destiny is much stronger, often to a comical level. Somebody like Lee Iacocca seems to believe that he personally rescued the Chrysler Corporation. The government's bailout had nothing to do with it; the rescue came about through his agency. In writing *The Road from Coorain* I thought it was important to relate the story of a young woman taking charge of her life in an unromantic way, in which it's perfectly clear that she arrives at a moment of choice. Telling that story seems to have fulfilled a big need for readers of the book.

Still another motivation that's very complex, but very important to me, is that we need a more inclusive rhetoric for feminism today. The different wings of the movement have become so politicized over issues like abortion and pornography, or over competing versions of feminist theory or literary criticism or social analysis, that feminists have become almost like the historians of my era as an academic. They're writing for a very small audience about very fine points. That rhetoric doesn't speak emotionally to a larger audience. Feminism can never succeed as a majority movement unless it can persuade a lot of men to become feminists. It can never succeed if it continues to proclaim the separate female utopia that's part of so much female-written science fiction today. We have to live in the world with men, and we have to convince them that it's morally right and just to treat women as equals. We need a rhetoric that also speaks to men. In retrospect, I suppose it was good training for me to talk to all those congressional committees when I was a college president.

Finally, I'm very much opposed to the current sentimental school of female psychology, which argues that women never separate from their families of birth because they bond with their same-sex parent and never develop boundaries that separate them from the primal mother. Proponents of this school of thought argue that women are always lodged in networks of female relationships and are therefore morally better than men, who possess an isolated, individualized psyche. I think that's wrong for a great variety of reasons. Our culture encourages men to talk about separating and encourages women to suppress the experience. I see men lodged in networks of supporting relationships everywhere I go. They don't come home and say, "I never could have gotten through the day at the office without Tom or Bill," but in fact they have many ways in which they display affection or support for each other — a hug or a pat on the shoulder. Women don't get to watch them doing that, so they're not aware of it.

So I wanted to write a story about separation — as honest an account as I could give of that process. My new memoir, *True North*, pursues that motif of separation. It's my personal testament in opposition to the sentimental school of thought about women. The view of women as always lodged in family networks is very attractive to the political right because it provides a good reason for keeping women from establishing a strong independent identity of their own. It also suggests that they won't form political bonds or aspire to life in the so-called "public sphere."

Both my brother and I have extraordinarily vivid visual memories. When we try to remember an event or an occasion, we start with where the chairs were in the room and what time of day it was and what the background noises were, and we re-create it. As a grader of papers I'm death on plagiarists because I can see the page where I once read that text. I have the artist's ability to see something, but I have no ability to translate it into a representation except through words. I've also been helped in determining the shape of my narrative by the larger social concerns that I've just described. And as a college administrator I have been studied at different stages of my career by psychologists who want to understand women leaders who are unusual in their generation — what experiences made me an activist and a leader. I can't tell you how many questionnaires I've filled out. Doing that naturally makes you reflect about what were important experiences in your life.

That in turn raises the question, when you actually write your memoir, of what to put in and what to leave out. As I said, I knew I had to get back to the personal style I had as a girl — that only exploring deeply-felt inner experience was going to do it for me. The danger is that in telling your life story you'll hurt some people's feelings. I couldn't have written *The Road from Coorain* while my mother was living. She would have struck me dead — not literally, but. . . . As far as others were concerned, except where I concealed someone's identity I showed my manuscript to the people I was writing about and let them say whether it was appropriate or not, or whether they minded. I've done the same thing with *True North*; I sent the pertinent pages to everybody in the book. I think it's an invasion of privacy not to. If you're going to see yourself in print you deserve a chance to correct anything that may be wrong.

Obviously the person who would be most concerned in *The Road from Coorain* was my brother. I sent him the first four chapters and said, "I won't publish this if you find it too painful." He called me up at four o'clock in the morning, because he had just finished reading it in Australia, and he said, "It's wonderful. Keep going. I had forgotten so much." The places of childhood are always etched on the memory with great power and clarity. I had been thinking about *The Road from Coorain* for a long time; it was already written in my head. (Expatriates always think about their life up to the point of departure.) It also helped that as an undergraduate in Australia I had been interested in getting people to understand Australian history from the point of view of someone who looked at the landscape and didn't see what was left out, because it wasn't like England or the rest of Europe, but who took it on its own terms. I wrote children's books and school textbooks that were histories of the settlement of Australia, and in doing so I honed my strong visual sense of landscape.

What's difficult and exhausting about writing as honest a memoir as you can, I think, is going back as a historian and, instead of just weltering in all those emotions, trying to think, "Why did it happen that way? What was really going on?" All the things you took as a given when you were a child you now have to reconstruct and experience from the point of view of many other people. For example, the thing I found hardest but most illuminating was trying to figure out how my parents were relating to each other in that period of great stress — the seven-year drought that killed everything they had built together as sheep farmers and that also finally killed my father. As a child they're just beings; they're your parents. To try to work through those events later in the persona of my father and my mother, understanding their personalities and temperaments, was painful but very instructive. Why didn't she understand how anxious he was? Why didn't he tell her, or was he not able to? What are the effects of social isolation and social deprivation?

I was anxious to re-create my mother in three dimensions, as large as life as I could get her, because she's such an extraordinary character. And what happened to her in the second half of her life is such a tragedy, so dreadfully sad, that I wanted not to shortchange her in any way. Today people ask me how I learned to manage my time so efficiently. I learned it by observing my mother when I was young. Although she had three children, she taught us school, eventually did all the cooking and cleaning at the sheep station, had a huge garden that fed us and many other people, and still had four hours a day free to read. She just never wasted a second. So as a child I had as a mother this wonderful, competent, loving, nurturing woman who was a tower of strength and creativity. Nothing fazed her; she was courageous to an extreme degree.

But first she lost my father and then she lost her eldest son, both in tragic accidents — in my father's case, a possible suicide. The loss of those paired male figures took root in her psyche, and as an older woman she became terribly dependent on her two remaining children and also on alcohol and tranquilizers, which, over an extended period, begin to affect the brain. She became subject to all kinds of paranoid delusions and turned into a punishing, angry, negative, and destructive person. The dramatic tension for me as a writer involved portraying this strong woman as seen through the eyes of the child who finally has to separate from her or lose her own life.

An outsider might put much of the blame for her tragic life on the hostile environment of the sheep station. But I didn't want to write that story, which is the Australian archetype. It comes out of the British colonial experience, which represents life in Australia as a battle with harsh elements. Of course that's a British imperial perspective; aboriginals don't experience Australia that way. It's a very bountiful land if you know how to live in it, and very beautiful. So I tried hard to evoke its beauty and the sense of the plenitude of nature when the seasons smile. True, the continent has these recurring periods of intense drought, but the natural vegetation is perfectly adapted to that. What created the disaster in my family history was not the land and the environment, but the introduction by white settlers of sharp-hoofed animals, which destroy and degrade the environment.

So the land is meant to be a character in *The Road from Coorain*, and it continues to be a character in *True North*, which is about my coming to North America. Today I work at M.I.T. in the Program on Science, Technology and Society, where a group of us are studying ways in which the humanities can contribute to an awareness and a thoughtful understanding of environmental issues. Much environmental thought nowadays is semifascist and authoritarian, going back to the fascist idea of people being rooted in blood in the soil and needing to relate in a very possessive way to a specific natural environment. A great deal of environmental writing has this cast, particularly in Russia; the myth of Mother Russia has always been a source of authoritarian political ideas. Ecofeminism is also raising a supposed female myth involving female-ruled prehistorical societies in which nature was the object of worship and which also — from what records we have — were highly authoritarian.

I'm interested in how one can look at the narrative treatment of nature to analyze and understand the political assumptions behind it. E. M. Forster's *A Passage to*

India, for instance, has a totally imperialist view of the Indian landscape — the Malabar caves. From reading the book you'd never know what the Indian history of those caves was, or what the Indian culture was. You can read American narratives about wildfires, which take those fires to be some terrible wickedness or catastrophe in nature, whereas burning is how many natural woods replenish themselves. So in my writing I try to make the natural environment a character — an instructive one, but not a sentimental one. In our work at M.I.T. I think it's important for us to understand how these arid, very delicate environments like Australia are misrepresented in European-style art and literature; almost every European assumption about climate and nature is wrong. But I'm not someone who wants to preserve unspoiled nature. It doesn't exist. Nature is a cultural construct, and we have to understand that it's a category that we must be critical of, just as we would be critical in analyzing any other category of thought. I'm not eager to return us to the wooden plow or Stone Age culture. Technology is a creation of the human intellect that we need to manage and understand.

When I first set out to write my memoir about growing up in Australia, I found that my memory was of all the painful things. But in the process of telling that story I rediscovered so much that was beautiful about my childhood. My brother had the same experience; he said my book reminded him of happy experiences that had been overwhelmed by later tragedy. Often there is a human tendency to obliterate happiness — to live in one's painful memories. But for me, going through my life gave me back the good things I had forgotten, and I've captured them for good. It gave me back my happy mother.

The book has also been helpful to other people. I can tell from my mail that it strikes a universal theme for women readers of all ages. It resonates for them because it's the story of a woman who takes charge of her life. I've also had an extensive correspondence with male readers of all ages. Many of them are the sons of single mothers, and they felt the same overwhelming sense of obligation to an all-provident female figure that I felt in relation to my mother. That correspondence has alerted me to a developmental concern for males that I hadn't been aware of. The mother-daughter relationship is traditionally sentimentalized but it's a trap, for sons as well as daughters — a trap because few people think honestly about the dimensions of misused maternal power. But the older men who write to me say that dealing honestly with exploitation by mothers is not an exclusively female problem. I've also had a great many letters from expatriates — the book made them feel at peace with having left — and many letters from Latin American readers, especially in the Argentine and Brazil. The way of life in the Australian outback is comparable to life on the pampas.

All of us live with a life history in our mind, and very few of us subject it to critical analysis. But we are storytelling creatures. So it's very important to examine your own story and make sure that the plot is the one you really want. When I give talks as a historian about the dominance of the romantic plot in women's telling of their life histories, I'm amused to see women investment bankers and corporate lawyers giving a wry smile, as if to say, "It's true — that's how I *do* see my life." As a young person it's important to scrutinize the plot you've internalized and find out whether it accurately represents what you want to be, because we tend to act out those life plots unless we think about them. I'm impatient with the postmodern effort to obfuscate the validity of narrative. We are time-bound creatures. We experience life along a time continuum; things happen sequentially in our lives, and we need to understand the causation. But we never really do understand it until we sit down and try to tell the story.

So I would say to young people: First, if you approach writing about your life honestly, you'll find a style of writing that you will never otherwise discover. And second, that process can take parents or other figures who seem larger than life and reduce them to people in your story. I recently visited an experimental inner-city elementary school in a slum area of Miami that had been devastated by the hurricane. I was struck by the fact that children eight or nine or ten years old, who had been having difficulty with English, were being asked to tell their story as though it was a television series. Some of their stories were so lively and so funny that the children were laughing, although the events themselves were quite grim. And I thought, what a genius that teacher was, because television is a genre they all know about, and they were telling stories about their families in a way that must have been wonderfully helpful to them.

Until you put people in your narrative you haven't quite

got them under control. The standard postmodern critique of narrative says that the narrator imposes by his or her own authority a certain meaning on the ebb and flow of events: that you change the story by where you begin it and end it, and that you impose your own meaning on events that's different from the meaning everybody else in the story puts on those events. In fact, Westerners have created a whole concept of the Asian or the African by the way we have told the history of their continents.

So there are many good things about the postmodern insistence that there is no meta-narrative. There is no fixed history, no history that is true. There are stories that we tell from our history, and we tell them well or we tell them ill. If you want to tell the history of the world in 1492, we Westerners talk about Columbus, but if you're from the Arab world a very different series of events is important. In the West we have written our history as if the West were the center of the world and the events that happened elsewhere are peripheral. Still, there's no reason not to try to be more inclusive. In the case of *The Road from Coorain*, it's my story, and anybody who reads it may deconstruct it any way they like. It's also quite conceivable that if I were to write about my childhood as an old woman in my eighties I would tell it differently. What matters is how I thought about it at the time I wrote it.

The young women I got to know when I was at Smith were energetically interested in writing and understanding themselves and their current life experiences. Their problem was that most of the narratives they saw, which were on television, were structured around very brief two-

or three-minute incidents. These women had never become accustomed to writing reflective expository prose — looking at an event and reflecting on what it means — because events on television are so neatly packaged that you don't think about the alternatives. One of my motives for writing *True North* now, rather than ten years from now, say, is that many memoirs have recently been written by women of my generation in the feminist movement who talk about how exhausting their experience of the movement was. That wasn't my experience at all. My life has been enlarged and enriched and strengthened by the feminist struggle, and I have been the gainer in every respect. Much of the current writing in women's studies stresses the problems of bias that women experience. If I were a girl in college today, reading all this stuff would be a real downer. For me, fighting bias has been energizing, and on the whole I've enjoyed it. Getting in a good honest rage about injustice isn't bad for you.

I was also prompted to write *True North*, which is about my life in North America, by the reaction of Australians to *The Road from Coorain*. They think much more about expatriation than other readers do. But I've come to believe that the notion of expatriation is a nineteenth-century creation. It comes out of the obsession of the male citizens with the national soil and territory. Historically, nobody ever bothered about women being required to change countries; they were meant to be able to shift allegiance overnight through marriage. It's been interesting for me as a set of political reflections to think about what it means to move to another country and another culture and another climate and another continent. The theme of *True North* is my experience of intellectual life in North America and finding a life partner who is my emotional and moral compass point. It's about exploring the Northern Hemisphere. The book ends in 1975, when I'm driving out of Toronto and around Lake Ontario to cross the border and go to Smith. Some readers have asked why I also didn't include my experiences as president of Smith in the book. I think you have to be at least twenty years away from what you write about to have the necessary detachment. Many memoirs or autobiographies get very cluttered in their later chapters because people don't know what was really involved. It takes more time to know what the shape of your life has been like.

Bibliography

In planning both editions of *Inventing the Truth*, it occurred to us that we would like to know what books our authors consulted or remembered or somehow found helpful in writing their own memoirs. We asked them for an informal list of their favorite first-person narratives or other works that influenced them. This bibliography is their answer to our request.

RUSSELL BAKER

Here are some of the books that were valuable to me during the writing of *Growing Up:*

Not So Wild a Dream by Eric Sevareid (Atheneum, 1976), *Personal History* by Vincent Sheean (Doubleday, Doran & Co., 1936), and *In Search of History* by Theodore H. White (Harper & Row, 1978). All three are journalists' memoirs distinguished by a great deal of frankness about their childhoods and private lives. After thirty-three years as a newspaperman I had trouble writing candidly about my "personal history" and found encouragement to try it anyhow in these fine books by three of our best journalists.

Exiles (Farrar, Straus & Giroux, 1970) and *Passage to Ararat* (Farrar, Straus & Giroux, 1975), both by Michael J. Arlen. The prose is so good that I couldn't help writing a little better after reading them. The books are models of how to write about sensitive family relationships and the most private emotions without falling into squalor and vulgarity.

The Dream of Golden Mountains by Malcolm Cowley (Viking Press, 1980) and *Starting Out in the Thirties* by Alfred Kazin (Little, Brown, 1965). Because I wanted to create a sense of what the Great Depression meant to adults and had only a child's memory of it, I looked for memoirs by people who had been adults in the 1930s. These were two of the best. Because they dealt with an urban, intellectual America totally different from anything I'd been aware of in the 1930s, they helped me understand the simplicity of the world of my childhood.

Because so much of the book would be about my parents' generation, which came to maturity during World War I and the Jazz Age, I looked for material that would convey a sense of how that period might have shaped people. The best of it included:

Exile's Return by Malcolm Cowley (Viking Press, 1934; revised, 1951) and *The Twenties* by Edmund Wilson (Farrar, Straus & Giroux, 1975), with their picture of New York's literary Bohemia. It was startling to be reminded that the twentieth century was already blazing away so furiously just 250 miles north of the rustic backwater where my family was still living so close to the nineteenth.

The Mauve Decade by Thomas Beer (Alfred A. Knopf, 1926) was valuable in helping me understand the social tyranny exercised by women during the 1890s, when my mother was born, and how that tradition might have been passed on to her.

Bibliography

Goodbye to All That by Robert Graves (Jonathan Cape, 1929), *The Great War and Modern Memory* by Paul Fussell (Oxford University Press, 1975), and *Memoirs of an Infantry Officer* (Faber & Faber, 1930) and *Sherston's Progress* (Faber & Faber, 1936), both by Siegfried Sassoon, are invaluable to an understanding of how World War I shattered the nineteenth-century sensibility and prepared us for twentieth-century brutality.

The Rise of Theodore Roosevelt by Edmund Morris (Coward, McCann & Geoghegan, 1979) conveys a marvelous sense of the optimism that characterized the American spirit before World War I and makes it easier to understand how devastating the Great Depression must have been to adults born at the start of the century.

Not having written much in a personal vein until I started the book, I read many books to see how the thing was done, to see if I could discover the trick, as it were. The best of these were:

Dispatches by Michael Herr (Alfred A. Knopf, 1977), a report from Vietnam by a man trapped inside a nightmare. This extraordinarily personal piece of war reporting triumphs because the writer is scrupulously honest about his own terror, fatigue, ignorance, cowardice and anger.

Happy Days, 1880–1892 (Alfred A. Knopf, 1940) and *Newspaper Days, 1899–1906* (Alfred A. Knopf, 1941) by H. L. Mencken. Mencken does it like nobody else. As I discovered after several false starts, though, if you try to do it Mencken's way, you will produce only a very inferior counterfeit.

The Years with Ross by James Thurber (Little, Brown, 1959). Thurber wrote better than almost anybody, and I believe writers should always read their betters. It reminds them that they're not quite as good as they think they are.

Roughing It (F. G. Gilman & Co., 1872) and *Life on the Mississippi* (J. S. Osgood & Co., 1883) by Mark Twain. Nobody understood better than Twain that a memoir is not biography, but an art form. What a pleasure to watch him improve dull stretches of arid fact with inventions of the mind. I also discovered that even the greatest writer can be defeated by insensate demands of editors. The last half of *Life on the Mississippi* is heavy going because an editor wanted it to be twice as long as it should have been.

Autobiography by Anthony Trollope (Williams & Norgate Ltd., 1887). Looking for tips from the most relentless writer ever, I found only advice to write relentlessly. It is, however, a fascinating look at a literary life built on the work ethic, and a valuable book for all writers to know about. When asked, "How can I become a writer?" I now reply, "Read Trollope's autobiography; the secret is there."

Autobiography (various versions have appeared under different titles from c. 1791) by Benjamin Franklin. I intended to write about this in the book and wanted to know if it was as hard to stay awake through as it was in my childhood. The answer was: not quite.

Remembrance of Things Past (Bernard Grasset, vol. I; La Nouvelle Revue Française, vols. II–VII, 1914–1927; Holt & Co., 1922; Random House, 1932) by Marcel Proust. This is the ultimate memoir. Proust's ability to startle the reader with some revelatory scene that suddenly casts everything in a new light is a gift I envy. I read through all seven very long volumes again in search of the secret. I had a wonderful time, while learning that I might just possibly achieve Proust's effects if I wrote seven very long volumes, though it was unlikely. So I wrote only one rather short volume.

ANNIE DILLARD

These are some first-person narratives I dearly love:

NINETEENTH-CENTURY UNITED STATES

The Education of Henry Adams (Houghton Mifflin, 1918). I like its vigorous thought and its assumption that an account of one's intellectual life is indeed an account of one's life.

Henry David Thoreau, *Walden* (Ticknor & Fields, 1854). In its formal shapeliness and metaphorical, hyperbolic prose it far exceeds the scrapbook journals as the monument of Thoreau the artist.

Richard Henry Dana, *Two Years Before the Mast* (Harper & Brothers, 1840).

Mark Twain, *Life on the Mississippi* (J. S. Osgood & Co., 1883).

TWENTIETH-CENTURY UNITED STATES

Alfred Kazin, *A Walker in the City* (Harcourt, Brace, 1951). This stirringly illustrates a paradox on which, I think, the finest auto-biographical literature depends, that is, that the life of the spirit, which in an adult often becomes the life of the mind, enters the child through the senses. I have read this book over and over again.

Russell Baker, *Growing Up* (Congdon & Weed, 1982). Most of the best memoirs, like this vivid and genial one, refrain from examining the self at all.

James McConkey, *Court of Memory* (Dutton, 1983). A recent and elegiac account of a calm life lived deeply. I admire its structural integrity and literary intelligence. More and more I find these aesthetic satisfactions in nonfiction; essayists and other nonfiction writers are taking the care and perhaps practicing the artifices that English prose writers used to practice in the seventeenth century. Many fiction writers whose work sees print apparently are not.

Mary Heaton Vorse, *Time and the Town: A Provincetown Chronicle* (Dial Press, 1942). Like Marjorie Kinnan Rawlings's *Cross Creek* (Charles Scribner's Sons, 1942) in its broad-spirited recreation of energetic and hospitable decades among friends.

The Autobiography of Malcolm X (Grove Press, 1965). A magnificent narrative.

Norman MacLean, *A River Runs Through It* (University of Chicago Press, 1976). Published as fiction, this reads like the best of memoirs. It is a favorite of many writers.

Lewis Thomas, *The Youngest Science* (Oxford University Press, 1983). The genial medical researcher remembers the medicine of his father's day and the researches of his own. A matter-of-fact quality to his writing and a pure, clean attention to the materials at hand make Lewis Thomas's writing modest, honest and serious.

Frank Conroy, *Stop-Time* (Viking Press, 1967). Conroy masters a narrative, dramatic, novelistic handling of scenes.

Booker T. Washington, *Up from Slavery* (Doubleday, Page & Co., 1901). This classic holds up; it is a pleasure to read.

Henry Beston, *The Outermost House* (Doubleday, Doran & Co., 1928). This Cape Cod masterpiece is broad and simple. Its power derives from two images: the cold, pagan stars and the fateful, killing waves.

Maureen Howard, *Facts of Life* (Little, Brown, 1978). Howard grew up in Bridgeport, Connecticut, among a variety of colorful people she describes with insight.

Maxine Hong Kingston, *The Woman Warrior* (Alfred A. Knopf, 1976). There is a long story in here about a Chinese

aunt that is one of the funniest stories I've seen in print. Kingston is a sophisticated and original writer.

Thomas Merton, *The Seven Storey Mountain* (Harcourt, Brace,
1948). Merton's account of the steps that led him from a privileged childhood in France, through Columbia University and
to a Trappist monastery in Kentucky.

James Thurber, *My Life and Hard Times* (Harper & Brothers,
1933). This is vintage Thurber.

Ethel Waters, *His Eye Is on the Sparrow* (Doubleday, 1951).
The singer Ethel Waters tells her moving story of music, hardship and faith.

Kate Simon, *Bronx Primitive* (Viking Press, 1982). A vivid,
rough-and-tumble childhood in a Bronx immigrant neighborhood in the 1930s.

AND ABROAD

John Cowper Powys, *Autobiography* (John Lane, 1934). An extreme of the genre, written with the usual Powys restrictions.
In this case he belabors his so-called eroticism and omits all
mention of the women in his life. The oddest of this great
writer's many odd books.

Edwin Muir, *An Autobiography* (Hogarth Press, 1954). A beautiful evocation of the timelessness of early childhood, in the Ork-
ney Islands, by the poet and translator of Kafka.

Ved Mehta, *Vedi* (Oxford University Press, 1982). In beautiful, formal, vivid language, the writer describes his blind, vigorous boyhood in India.

Kildare Dobbs, *Running to Paradise* (Oxford University Press,
1962). The Canadian man of letters recounts his travels and
impressions following his immigration from Northern Ireland.

Nikos Kazantzakis, *Report to Greco* (Simon & Schuster, 1965).

This strong, storyteller's autobiography escapes the usual hazards of Kazantzakis.

Maxim Gorky, the trilogy: *My Childhood* (T. W. Laurie, 1915); *My Apprenticeship* (Foreign Languages Publishing House, 1952, also as *In the World*, The Century Co., 1917); *My Universities* (Boni & Liveright, 1923). Gorky's childhood was actually colorful; his father was a dyer, and the dye vats in the yard stained everything. The usual Russian extremes of living and of writing are right here.

Graham Greene, *A Sort of Life* (Bodley Head, 1971). An austere, intelligent autobiography.

Pablo Neruda, *Memoirs* (Farrar, Straus & Giroux, 1977). The poet writes a muscular prose; he describes the literary camaraderie of his early manhood in Valparaíso.

C. S. Lewis, *Surprised by Joy* (Harcourt Brace Jovanovich, 1955). The Christian's intellectual autobiography begins with a happy boyhood.

Wilfrid Sheed, *Frank and Maisie* (Simon & Schuster, 1985). His parents were low-church British evangelists, great and lively characters.

Vladimir Nabokov, *Speak, Memory* (Putnam, 1966). Nabokov's memoir of old Russia is pure description, emotional in its spareness. He describes a needlepoint chair seat.

Jean-Paul Sartre, *The Words* (Gallimard, 1964; George Braziller, 1964). Sartre's original memoir is, I think, his best, most literary work.

Antoine de Saint-Exupéry, *Wind, Sand and Stars* (Gallimard, 1939; Reynal & Hitchcock, 1939). In the early days of aviation the author flew the mails over North Africa. A dandy book.

ALFRED KAZIN

Because of the Puritan passion for constantly keeping in mind the report of one's doings and misdemeanors to be delivered to Almighty God, American writing is especially rich in journals and memoirs from the earliest period. The journals of Ralph Waldo Emerson (Houghton Mifflin, 1909–1914); Henry David Thoreau, one of the longest ever kept (Houghton Mifflin, 1906); Walt Whitman's *Specimen Days* (Donald McKay, 1882); John Quincy Adams's diaries, sometimes called "Memoirs" and supposed to be the longest journal ever kept by a public man (J. B. Lippincott & Co., 1874–1877), are all conscious autobiographies in this sense.

I have been preoccupied much of my life with this literature, probably because I have kept a journal since I was in knee pants, and because my interest in American literature keeps returning to the "personal" — by which I mean "the self as history."

American classics in this context: *The Education of Henry Adams* (Houghton Mifflin, 1918) — to me the most wonderful example of how to see one's life as history.

Earlier, of course, *The Autobiography of Benjamin Franklin*, the prototypical story of the self-made American, but distinctive also for its wry humor.

Theodore Dreiser's *Dawn* (Horace Liveright, 1931). There is nothing else like it for portraying the "provincial" seizing for wonder and literary inspiration upon the "Big City" (Chicago).

Hemingway's *A Moveable Feast* (Charles Scribner's Sons, 1964). Full of lies or shall we say delusions, but marvelous nonetheless because it shows the same artifice of genius that went to make up his classic short stories.

Moving about at random, I would also include Malcolm X's

Autobiography (Grove Press, 1965). I am aware that he had a lot of "help" in this, to put it gently, but it is the best story I know of the black experience in America from a purely personal, sensory point of view. Though of course I have to add Richard Wright's *Black Boy* (Harper & Brothers, 1945). Wright remains in my mind the most gifted of all twentieth-century black American writers.

I have forgotten such central items in American autobiography as *The Autobiography of Lincoln Steffens* (Harcourt, Brace, 1931), a classic portrait of American politics, urban scandals and Steffens's own utopian self-delusions on the subject of Soviet Russia, which are now as funny as they are sad.

One can hardly omit from any table of American autobiography such succulent dishes as Whitman's *Leaves of Grass* (Fowler & Wells, 1855), Thoreau's *Walden* (Ticknor & Fields, 1854), Saul Bellow's *The Adventures of Augie March* (Viking Press, 1953) and *Herzog* (Viking *Press*, 1964), and Robert Lowell's *Life Studies* (Farrar, Straus & Cudahy, 1959). There is no need, perhaps, to go on in this vein — Sylvia Plath, James Merrill, Anne Sexton, etc., etc.

The prime example in modern European literature of the novel as autobiography, the autobiography as novel, is Proust's *Remembrance of Things Past*. Proust's great biographer, George Painter, said he documented much of his biography from the novel!

TONI MORRISON

As Toni Morrison points out in her talk, a large part of her literary heritage consists of the book-length narratives that were written by slaves in the eighteenth and nineteenth centuries. Well over a hundred were published, she says, and she names the ones that have been particularly important to her as a writer. She also mentions several influential books by modern writers such as Simone de Beauvoir and James Baldwin. Her talk is her bibliography.

EILEEN SIMPSON

The copy of Vladimir Nabokov's *Speak, Memory* (G. P. Putnam's Sons, 1966) that I was given as a Valentine's Day present in 1967 is dog-eared from many readings. It's the book I have most often recommended to students who are thinking of writing a memoir.

Other favorite memoir/autobiographies are Leo Tolstoy's *Childhood, Boyhood, Youth* (Penguin, 1964); Jean-Jacques Rousseau's *Confessions* (Penguin, 1953); Jean-Paul Sartre's *The Words* (Braziller, 1964); Charlie Chaplin, *My Autobiography* (Simon & Schuster, 1964); and Mary McCarthy's *Memoirs of a Catholic Girlhood* (Harcourt Brace Jovanovich, 1962). It is no accident that all the authors were orphans.

A writer who must sometimes have wished he were an orphan, Henry James, was very much a son and brother, as he writes in *Notes of a Son and Brother.*

Essential to my preparation for writing *Poets in Their Youth* was a rereading of the works of the men I was going to write about. The letters I received after the book was published that gave me the greatest pleasure were those that said my book had sent the reader back to the poems of Robert Lowell, John Berryman, Delmore Schwartz, Randall Jarrell, and the others.

Also useful were the poets' books of criticism, particularly John Berryman's *The Freedom of the Poet* (Farrar, Straus & Giroux, 1976).

The memoir/autobiography that was most helpful to me in living with the memory of my painful struggles to learn to read and spell was W. B. Yeats's *Autobiographies* (Macmillan and Co.,

Ltd., 1926), in which he writes feelingly about his academic failure as a schoolboy and his father's efforts to teach him to read.

IAN FRAZIER

In my research for *Family* I read books on all kinds of subjects. I have a high threshold of boredom when I'm reading for the sake of research, and often I would find myself deep in a text in which not much of interest had turned up for days. Luckily, the opposite experience — coming upon a book essential to my research that was also interesting and well written and fun to read — happened regularly, too. In this bibliography I'll confine myself to books of the second sort. Readers interested in a fuller bibliography may consult the notes at the end of *Family*.

Because an ancestor of mine is mentioned briefly in *A Half-Century of Conflict,* the ninth volume of the historian Francis Parkman's ten-volume *France and England in North America* (1899), I read the entire history, volumes I–X. I think Parkman is the greatest American historian, but what I really like him for is the incidentals: his Yankee prejudices, his affectionate and unsparing view of the Iroquois, and especially his landscapes. The Great Lakes as the first French explorers saw them, he says, were "wilderness oceans stretching beneath the sky."

Black Cargoes: A History of the Atlantic Slave Trade 1518–1865, by Daniel P. Mannix in collaboration with Malcolm Cowley (1962), is an interesting account of an overlooked (and horrible) part of American history. Sharks followed slave ships waiting for the dead and the dying to be thrown overboard. Captured Africans desperately clawed at the beaches as they were dragged to the boat; beneath the clear water of African slave-ship ports, the bottoms of the harbors were white with bones.

An excellent account of life on the Midwestern frontier is *The*

Old Northwest Pioneer Period 1815–1840, by Roscoe Carlyle Buley (1950). In its notes I found many good primary sources to pursue.

For the heck of it I read Harriet Beecher Stowe's *Uncle Tom's Cabin* (1852). It is a preposterous, manipulative, gripping book, full of unexpectedly sharp period details — definitely worth a read, or a reread. To me, Simon Legree's plantation has much in common with the benighted housing projects of Brooklyn or the South Bronx. I also read or reread books by Thoreau, Melville, Whitman, and Hawthorne. If you know a little about nineteenth-century American history, especially religious history, these books are even more lively and interesting.

Of the primary sources on the frontier that I read, most were travel narratives by Easterners or Englishmen. I liked *Personal Narrative of Travels . . . 1817–1818*, by Elias Pym Fordham, and *Indiana Miscellany*, by Rev. William C. Smith (1867). Charles Dickens's *American Notes* (1842) is a must-read for a view of this period. What Dickens saw of the frontier seems to have appalled him.

It is said that more words have been written on the American Civil War than on any other subject except the Bible. Out of that torrent the wise reader will select Shelby Foote's three-volume *The Civil War: A Narrative* (1963), a panoramic, clear, and poetic history. On the subject of General Stonewall Jackson, Henry Kyd Douglas's *I Rode with Stonewall* (1940) is my favorite. It is the only actually funny book I know of about the war, and an American classic. *Life and Letters of General Thomas J. Jackson*, by his widow, Mary Anna Jackson (1892), is lively and sometimes moving in its account of the personal side of Jackson's life.

For the period between the end of the Civil War and the 1920s, I have already mentioned A. M. Schlesinger's *The Rise of the City* (1933). A more chaotic book, but an interesting one, is the two-volume *A History of the United States since the Civil War,* by Ellis P. Overholzer (1926–1931), full of details about the lawlessness in the South after the war's end, and about the Ku Klux Klan. Another historian who wrote a lot about this period is Allan Nevins; his *John D. Rockefeller: The Heroic Age of American Enterprise* (1940), though inclined to hagiography, is a good book about a fascinating man. I also liked *The History of the Telephone,* by Herbert N. Casson (1910).

Books about America's major shifts in population — from rural areas to the cities, and then from the cities to the suburbs — are *The Urbanization of America 1860–1915,* by Blake McKelvey (1963), and *Crabgrass Frontier: The Suburbanization of the United States,* by Kenneth T. Jackson (1985). Especially if you grew up in the suburbs, Jackson's book is great.

For the chapter in *Family* that talks about Lake Erie, I relied heavily on *Erie: The Lake that Survived,* by Noel M. Burns (1985), a technical book, but readable.

Much of my research had to do with the history of Protestantism in America. I began with a very good survey of the subject, *Righteous Empire: The Protestant Experience in America,* by Martin E. Marty (1970). To get the flavor of the disputatious religious scene in America in the first half of the nineteenth century I read books like *The Philosophy of Sectarianism: or, A Classified View of the Christian Sects of the United States,* by Rev. Alexander Blakie (1855); and *The Life of Our Blessed Lord and Saviour Jesus Christ,* by Rev. John Fleetwood (1822); and *Sectarianism Is Heresy,* by Rev. Andrew Wylie (1840). (I must admit that in those books I sometimes skimmed over the steeper parts.) I read Ralph Waldo Emerson's *Selected Essays* (edited by Larzer Ziff; 1982), in which the only time I was completely sure of my footing was in his remarkable essay on Napoleon; and

William James's *The Varieties of Religious Experience* (1902), a great book in which the text is interesting and the voluminous footnotes more interesting still. I have also mentioned *The American Religion: The Emergence of the Post-Christian Nation*, by Harold Bloom (1992). Bloom sees the history of religion in America in an original and fascinating way. To get an idea of twentieth-century trends in American religious thought, a reader might move from H. Richard Niebuhr's *The Kingdom of God in America* (1937), to a 1950s-era bestseller like Norman Vincent Peale's *The Power of Positive Thinking*, to *A Testament of Hope: The Essential Writings and Speeches of Martin Luther King, Jr.* (1986).

HENRY LOUIS GATES, JR.

I began to teach a course on the reading and writing of autobiography in the early eighties at Yale. Commencing with *Mandeville's Travels* and Augustine's *Confessions*, the students made their way through Rousseau and Benjamin Franklin, Frederick Douglass and Henry Adams, to Gertrude Stein, Alice James, Zora Neale Hurston, Nabokov's *Speak, Memory*, Sartre's *The Words*, and Soyinka's *Ake*. It was a "reading-into-writing" course, in which students imitated and parodied the forms of the autobiographers in the first half of the semester, then wrote in their own voices in the semester's second half. Most effective of all, perhaps, for learning how to make oneself a character in one's own narrative was the writing of an obituary in the first week of class, which each student had to read aloud before her or his fellow seminarians.

I also teach a course in African-American autobiography. In this tradition I am especially drawn to the slave narratives, especially those by Frederick Douglass (1845) and Harriet Jacobs (1861).

W.E.B. Du Bois's *The Souls of Black Folk*, consisting of lyrically autobiographical essays, is perhaps my favorite book, but I am also drawn to Richard Wright's *Black Boy*, James Baldwin's *Notes of a Native Son*, Maya Angelou's *I Know Why the Caged Bird Sings*, and *The Autobiography of Malcolm X*. Claude Brown's *Manchild in the Promised Land* moved me deeply as a teenager, as did Dick Gregory's *Nigger* and Sammy Davis, Jr.'s *Yes, I Can*.

I avidly read, and sometimes review, the autobiographies of my contemporaries. Among these, Lorene Cary's *Black Ice*, Brent Staple's *Parallel Time*, and Nathan McCall's *Makes Me Wanna Holler*, it seems to me, are superb. Nobel laureate Wole Soyinka's memoir of his boyhood, *Ake*, is a masterpiece. Among fictional memoirs, none is superior to *Annie John*, by Jamaica Kincaid.

JIL KER CONWAY

Jane Addams, *Twenty Years at Hull House*, Macmillan (1910). The classic American woman's autobiography describing education and the quest for an independent life.

Alice Hamilton, *Exploring the Dangerous Trades: The Autobiography of Alice Hamilton, M.D.* (Northeastern University Press, 1985). A less well known but delightful account of an American woman's education and professional life.

Anne Walker Fearn, *My Days of Strength* (Harper Bros., 1939). An American woman's narrative of self-discovery through professional education and life as a medical missionary in China.

A. B. Facey, *A Fortunate Life*. An extraordinary Australian narrative about the harshness of backcountry life for a lonely and exploited boy.

Mrs. Aenaes Gunn, *We of the Never Never*. A classic Australian narrative of isolation and endurance in the Northern Territory.

Sir Keith Hancock, *Country or Calling*. An Australian historian's account of the choice made between native land and intellectual vocation.

Emily Carr, *Klee Wyck*. (Clarke Irwin, 1965). A Canadian artist's description of the process by which she shed the British colonial view of Canada's landscape through studying the totems of Canada's West Coast Indians.

WILLIAM ZINSSER

Two of my favorite memoirs are by writers who gave talks in the original series: Russell Baker's *Growing Up* and Alfred Kazin's *A Walker in the City*. I've also long admired Jill Ker Conway's *The Road from Coorain* and Eileen Simpson's *Poets in Their Youth*. Here are a dozen others that I enjoyed with unusual intensity when I first encountered them and that I still remember vividly as models of the form.

Arlen, Michael J. *Exiles* (Farrar, Straus & Giroux, 1970). A stylish and sensitive recollection of a father and mother who were known on two continents for their glamour and of what it was like to be their son.

Behrman, S. N. *People in a Diary: A Memoir* (Little, Brown, 1972). An extraordinary gallery of famous friends — most memorably, the young Siegfried Sassoon and the dying George Gershwin — recalled with charm and warmth by Behrman from the diary he kept for fifty years.

Hart, Moss. *Act One* (Random House, 1959). One of America's most successful playwrights had a New York boyhood of such grinding poverty that the memory of it, as told here with a born dramatist's sense of timing and surprise, still haunts and troubles me.

Horgan, Paul. *Tracings: A Book of Partial Portraits* (Farrar, Straus & Giroux, 1993). A perfect example of the memoir in which a writer revisits his life through interesting people he has known. Vividly recalled over a span of more than seventy years are, among others, Vachel Lindsay, Feodor Chaliapin, Mary Garden, Somerset Maugham, Edmund Wilson, and Igor Stravinsky — as well as the person Paul Horgan was at the moment when their lives intersected with his.

Houseman, John. *Run-Through: A Memoir* (Simon & Schuster, 1972). The author's role as midwife to such innovative productions as the Virgil Thomson-Gertrude Stein opera *Four Saints in Three Acts*, the WPA's Negro Theatre Project and Orson Welles's Mercury Theatre and *Citizen Kane* is recalled with gusto and a remembered enjoyment of huge risks gladly taken.

Kidd, David. *Peking Story* (Clarkson N. Potter, Griffin paperback, 1988). The fond and observant memoir of a young American student in Peking who married a girl from an aristocratic Chinese family at the worst of times for such a union: the high tide of the Communist victory, in 1949, which brought a turbulent end to the four-thousand-year-old China and made Westerners unwelcome aliens in a hostile new land.

Mencken, H. L. *Happy Days, 1880–1892* (Alfred A. Knopf, 1940); *Newspaper Days, 1899–1906* (Knopf, 1941); and *Heathen Days, 1890–1936* (Knopf, 1943). These peppery memoirs, which I first found in Armed Forces Editions during World War II, brightened many long nights in North Africa and Italy with their exuberant style, reinforcing, among other things, my dream of becoming a newspaperman when the war was over. In 1980, twenty chapters from the three volumes were published in a book called *A Choice of Days* (Knopf), selected and introduced by Edward L. Galligan.

Mortimer, John. *Clinging to the Wreckage: A Part of a Life* (Ticknor & Fields, 1982). The son of a blind barrister who specialized in divorce cases whose lurid details had to be read aloud to him, Mortimer — a barrister himself and also a prolific author and playwright — has written a memoir that is both tender and hilarious.

Nabokov, Vladimir. *Speak, Memory* (Putnam, 1966). Although English was Nabokov's fourth language, no English or American author has written a more elegant memoir than this meticulous recollection of a golden childhood — a world of private tutors and summer houses — in czarist St. Petersburg.

Origo, Iris. *Images & Shadows: Part of a Life* (Harcourt Brace Jovanovich, 1971). The wise and graceful memoir of an American who grew up partly in Ireland and Europe, married an Italian, and created a life on a farm in Tuscany that had many fulfillments, not the least being the chance to hide Italian partisans and Allied soldiers during the Nazi occupation in World War II.

Pritchett, V. S. *A Cab at the Door* (Random House, 1968). Pritchett recalls a boyhood that was almost Dickensian in its hardship — his apprenticeship to the London leather trade belongs to the nineteenth century — without self-pity and even with a certain merriment and gratitude. A wonderful memoir.

Woolf, Leonard. *Growing: An Autobiography of the Years 1904–1911* (Harcourt, Brace & World, 1962). The second of an eventual six memoirs by the man Virginia Woolf would marry. This volume is my favorite because it compresses one man's exotic experience — Woolf's years as a young British civil servant in a village in Ceylon — and by extension tells the story of all the earnest colonials who have found themselves trying to administer justice in strange and bewildering lands.

Contributors

RUSSELL BAKER was born in rural Virginia in 1925, spent two years training as a Navy flier in World War II, graduated from Johns Hopkins University in 1947, and began his newspaper career with the Baltimore *Sun*. In 1954 he joined the *New York Times* and covered the White House, the Senate, the State Department, and several presidential campaigns before starting his Pulitzer Prize–winning column, "Observer," in 1962. He has published twelve books, including *The Good Times*, a memoir about the glory of being a young newspaperman in the golden-age America of the 1950s. He is host of the PBS television program *Masterpiece Theatre* and lives with his wife, Miriam, in northern Virginia near the village where he was born.

ANNIE DILLARD was born in 1945 in Pittsburgh. She is the author of ten books, including *An American Childhood* and *The Living*, a novel about nineteenth-century Puget Sound. Her most recent book, *Mornings Like This*, is, she says, "a kind of found poetry." In 1975 her *Pilgrim at Tinker Creek* won the

Pulitzer Prize for nonfiction. Her writing appears in *The Atlantic, Harper's, Yale Review,* and other magazines. Her many awards include fellowship grants from the Guggenheim Foundation and the National Endowment for the Arts. In 1982 she delivered the Phi Beta Kappa oration at the commencement exercises of Harvard University. She lives in Middletown, Connecticut, with her family.

ALFRED KAZIN was born in Brooklyn, graduated from the City College of New York, and began his career in 1942 as literary editor of *The New Republic.* Between 1963 and 1985 he was Distinguished Professor of English at the State University of New York in Stony Brook and at the City University of New York Graduate Center. He has also been a visiting professor at many universities here and abroad. His books include three memoirs — *A Walker in the City, Starting Out in the Thirties,* and *New York Jew* — and such classics of literary criticism as *On Native Grounds* and *An American Procession.* He has edited anthologies and critical studies of such writers as Emerson, Melville, Hawthorne, Henry James, and Stephen Crane. He is a member of the American Academy and Institute of Arts and Letters.

TONI MORRISON was born in Lorain, Ohio, graduated from Howard University, and received her master's degree from Cornell. For twenty years she was a senior editor at Random House. She has taught at many universities, including Yale, Rutgers, Stanford, the State University of New York, and the University of Michigan, and since 1989 has been Robert F. Goheen Professor in the Council of the Humanities at Princeton. Her six major novels, *The Bluest Eye, Sula, Song of Solomon, Tar Baby, Beloved,* and *Jazz,* have received wide acclaim, including the 1988 Pulitzer Prize for *Beloved.* She is a member of the American Academy and Institute of Arts and Letters and a trustee of the New York Public Library. In 1993 she was awarded the Nobel Prize for Literature.

EILEEN SIMPSON was born in New York and graduated from Hunter College. She was married soon afterward to the poet John Berryman and lived mainly in Princeton. She received a graduate degree in psychology from New York University, became a member of the psychology department at Rutgers University, and subsequently opened her own practice as a psychotherapist. After her remarriage in 1960 she lived in Paris, where she began to write short stories. Since returning to New York in the mid-'60s she has divided her time between her writing and her clinical practice. She has published short stories in the *Transatlantic Review* and other magazines. She is the author of a novel, *The Maze,* three memoirs — *Reversals, Poets in Their Youth,* and *Orphans* — and a nonfiction book, *Late Love.*

IAN FRAZIER was born in 1951. He grew up in Hudson, Ohio, and attended Harvard College. In 1974 he became a staff writer for *The New Yorker,* to which he continues to contribute essays, reporting pieces, and humor. In 1982 he moved to Montana to undertake research for *Great Plains,* which became a bestseller upon its publication in 1989. His other books include *Dating Your Mom,* a collection of humor pieces; *Nobody Better, Better than Nobody,* a collection of nonfiction articles; and *Family,* a memoir that interweaves the story of his parents and his Midwestern ancestors with the larger history of the United States. He now lives in Brooklyn with his wife and two children.

HENRY LOUIS GATES, JR., grew up in Piedmont, West Virginia. He graduated summa cum laude from Yale with a degree in history. He became a London correspondent for *Time* and received his Ph.D. in English from Cambridge University. He has taught at Yale, Cornell, and Duke and is now professor of English and chairman of the department of Afro-American Studies at Harvard. He writes extensively for such publications as *Harper's*, *The New York Times Book Review*, and *The New Yorker* and has edited and contributed to a wide variety of scholarly books and journals. His books include *Figures in Black; The Signifying Monkey: A Theory of Afro-American Literary Criticism*, for which he received an American Book Award; *Loose Canons*; and the memoir *Colored People*.

JILL KER CONWAY was born in New South Wales, Australia, the region described in her best-selling memoir *The Road from Coorain*. A graduate of the University of Sydney, she received her Ph.D. from Harvard and subsequently was vice president for internal affairs at the University of Toronto. In 1975 she became the first woman president of Smith College, serving in that position for ten years. Since then she has been a visiting scholar and professor at the Massachusetts Institute of Technology. She is a director of a number of major American companies and a trustee of several universities and foundations. Her other books include *Written by Herself*, an anthology of American women's autobiography, and *True North*, a continuation of her earlier memoir. She lives in Boston with her husband, the historian John Conway.

WILLIAM ZINSSER was born in New York and is a graduate of Princeton University. After serving overseas in the army in World War II he spent thirteen years on the *New York Herald Tribune* as an editor, writer, and critic. He left the paper in 1959 to become a freelance writer and has since written regularly for leading magazines. During the 1970s he taught nonfiction writing at Yale, where he was master of Branford College. His fifteen books include the bestseller *On Writing Well*, now in its fifth edition; *Writing to Learn; Willie and Dwike*, a portrait of the jazz musicians Willie Ruff and Dwike Mitchell; *Spring Training, American Places*, and *Speaking of Journalism*. He teaches at the New School, in New York, where he lives with his wife, Caroline Zinsser.